OPEN YOUR HEART

with Geocaching

"Adventure is closer than you think. This book is an insightful read about how geocaching literally brings adventure to your doorstep and how you can find life in those spaces and places we often overlook. As an avid backcountry skier, climber, hiker, and adventurer, I can honestly say that the 'outdoors' never looked so big and full of potential as they do now through the prospect of geocaching."

—Kendall Card, backcountry.com

"In a sea of 'How To' books, finally there is a 'Why To' book. Jeannette truly captures the joy and spirit of geocaching. This book doesn't just teach a new hobby, it reveals new tools for finding greater fulfillment and passion in our lives."

—Mary Votava, actor and singer, soprano.org.

OPEN YOUR HEART

with *Geocaching*

Mastering Life through Love of Exploration

JEANNETTE CÉZANNE

DreamTime Publishing, Inc.

DreamTime Publishing, Inc., books are available at special quantity discounts for bulk purchases for sales promotions, premiums, fund-raising, and educational needs. Please contact us at www.DreamTimePublishing.com for additional information.

Excerpt on page 3 from *The Phantom Tollbooth* by Norton Juster illustrated by Jules Feiffer, copyright © 1961 and renewed 1989 by Norton Juster; Illustrations copyright © 1961 and renewed 1989 by Jules Feiffer. Used by permission of Random House Children's Books, a division of Random House, Inc.

Excerpt on mysticism, page 80, from *Wishful Thinking: A Theological ABC* by Frederick Buechner. Copyright © 1973 by Frederich Buechner. Reprinted by permission of HarperCollins Publishers.

Library of Congress Cataloging-in-Publication Data

Cézanne, Jeannette.
   Open your heart with geocaching : mastering life through love of exploration / Jeannette Cézanne.
      p. cm.
   ISBN-13: 978-1-60166-004-6 (trade pbk. : alk. paper)
   1. Geocaching (Game) 2. Geocaching (Game)—Psychological aspects. I. Title.
   GV1202.G46C49   2007
   623.89—dc22

                                                                        2007006325

Branding, website, and cover design for DreamTime Publishing by
   Rearden Killion • www.reardenkillion.com
Illustrations by Janice Marie Phelps • www.janicephelps.com
Text layout and design by Gary A. Rosenberg • www.garyarosenberg.com

This publication is designed to provide accurate and authoritative information in regard to the subject matter covered. It is sold with the understanding that the publisher is not engaged in rendering legal, accounting, or other professional service. If legal advice or other expert assistance is required, the services of a competent professional person should be sought.
   —*From a declaration of principles jointly adopted by a committee of the American Bar Association and a committee of publishers.*

Readers should consult with a physician before undertaking any exercise, fitness, or diet program.

This book is printed on recycled, acid-free paper containing a minimum of 50% recycled, de-inked fiber.

Contents

Note from the Publisher

Balancing the overall mission of a series of books with each author's individual creativity and vision is an enjoyable and rewarding challenge. The goal of this note is to tie the loose ends together to make your experience with this book as meaningful as possible.

We have two goals with the Open Your Heart series. The first is to provide you with practical advice about your hobby or interest, in this case geocaching. We trust this advice will increase your ongoing enjoyment of geocaching, or even encourage you to explore a new activity.

Our second goal is to help you use what you know and love to make the rest of your life happier and easier. This process worked in different ways for each of our writers, so it will likely work in different ways for each of you. For some, it's a matter of becoming more self-aware. Just realizing what makes you happy while hunting for a new cache, and then gradually learning to use those feelings as a barometer when dealing with your job, relationships, and other issues could be an important first step. For others, geocaching provides an important outlet for stress and contemplation, allowing you to go back into your daily life refreshed. For yet others, you might discover how to meditate, how to connect with the mysterious flow of the Universe when you are immersed in geocaching. Once you recognize the beauty of that for what it is, you can then learn to connect with the flow in other ways at other times.

We are not suggesting you will find all of your answers in this book. We are, though, inviting you to look at something you love with new eyes, a new perspective, and a new heart. Once you recognize the importance of feeling good in one area of your life, you are open to feeling good in the rest of your life. And that is the cornerstone to mastering your life.

Happy reading!

Meg Bertini

Meg Bertini
Publisher

*This book is for all those who
want to open their hearts . . .
and especially for those who
don't know—yet—that they do.*

Acknowledgments

Thanks to the many people who touch my life, some of them daily, some of them sporadically, all of them deeply, with a sense of awe and beauty and insight and wisdom.

Thanks especially to my family, the people who are closest to my heart: Paul, Jacob, and Anastasia. Most of what is good in me is there either for or because of you.

Thanks also to Meg Bertini, friend, colleague, and publisher; to Julie Blackburn, for our forever-friendship; to Jon Arterton, for Sunday morning music and the Treehouse (and be sure to check him out as part of The Flirtations!); to my brother-in-law, John Czarnecki, for loving me anyway; to BigRock95, for my first geo-event; to Peter and Niamh for Guinness and a great local pub (the Shaskeen in Manchester); to MacKenzie, for more Guinness and another great local pub (the Squealing Pig in Provincetown); to Neil Rosen, for words and other lovely things; to Susan (Lillyflowers) Aufieri, for keeping some sanity in my life; to Carem Bennett, for all her thoughts and prayers and support; to Shauna Maggs of geocaching.com, for opening doors; and to Philip Spitzer and Lukas Ortiz, literary agents *extraordinaires*.

Belated thanks to Spike, the cat-of-my-dreams, who never went geocaching but who was always there for me when I came home. I miss you, *mon chat*.

Author's Note

This is not really a book about geocaching, although it's masquerading as one. There are already some terrific books out there about geocaching, and websites abound that will really equip you well to go out and pursue the hobby.

I have a different goal altogether: I want you to feel. To notice things. To pay attention. Geocaching isn't the end: it's the means to the end. I want you to use geocaching as a pleasant excuse to open your heart to the world around you.

So I've included a lot of information here that isn't part of most books about the hobby: thoughts, memories, quotations, strolls off onto tangents that may or may not eventually wander back to the main point.

In the same way, inevitably, I've left out a lot. A lot of the nuts-and-bolts. A lot of the specifics. I'm not going to be comparing brands of GPS receivers here. I'm not even going to teach you how to use a GPS receiver. There are people and places out there that do that far, far better than I ever could, and I've tried to include at least a decent sampling of them in the resources section at the end of the book.

You might even want to take a moment now and explore the

back of the book for some reassurance that there really is some "news you can use" here: check out the resources and the glossary (and you may wish to keep a bookmark in the glossary as you read, anyway, as there's some inevitable jargon to wade through).

I've also included a number of different voices here, some through interviews, some through quotations in passing, some through their writings. I wanted to be sure that we listened to a lot of different people on geocaching (and, for that matter, on opening one's heart) so that you'd have a fuller picture of the hobby and some of the people who do it. That's the best way to be introduced to anything—through the voices of those who love it.

If what I have to say here interests you, then explore some more. Visit the websites. Read the books. Think about whether this hobby might be a good fit for you. Don't use this as your sole guide, or you will end up lost somewhere. You might even end up *dead* somewhere. Use your common sense.

And maybe take this book along when you do start geocaching, to remind you of why you started in the first place.

Preface

Forests were the first temples of the Divinity, and it is in the
forests that men have grasped the first idea of architecture.

Francois-Rene de Chateaubriand (1768–1848)

Here's what happens.

Something—a person, an idea, an activity—finds its way, some-how, into your heart. It stays there, spreading warmth throughout your life, opening your spirit to the new joy and inspiration that has come to be living in your soul.

At some point what is in your heart passes into your mind, and it lives there for a while, too. You think about it, turning it over and over again like a polished pebble, like a worry-stone. You incorporate it into your rational being just as it has been incorporated into your spiritual being, making it truly become a part of you.

And then, finally, you feel compelled to share it, to move it beyond yourself, to make it part of your life in the community. And so it moves back through your heart—because sharing comes from the heart, not the head—and when it does that, it changes you forever.

All of the books in the *Open Your Heart* series speak of this truth. My heart has been opened and my life enriched by many things in the world, by some people, by certain activities, by an occasional flash of ecstasy, by one moment of perfect beauty. I am grateful for all of them.

In choosing to write about geocaching, I have not turned my back on the many other activities that have opened and that continue to open my heart. I have chosen this one because it is within everyone's reach, can fit into any schedule, takes no particular talent or inclination, and requires no more commitment than any one person is willing to make. It requires access to a computer and a GPS receiver; but both are within the means of most people reading this book. It can take place anywhere in the world, in extreme conditions and in pleasant parks, involve intense physical activity or as little effort as one wishes to expend.

In other words, it is Everyman's (and Everywoman's!) opportunity to try something that will challenge them to open their hearts as mine has been opened.

I invite you to try. To see if this activity is one that opens your heart. If not geocaching, then one of the other activities in the DreamTime series. Explore them all. Appropriate what seems good and right for *your* life.

Because the opening of our hearts is what helps us become part of the world around us, part of the community that enriches us, part of the activities and people and wisdom that make us whole.

Jeannette Cézanne
October, 2006 • Provincetown, Massachusetts

Foreword

I f it wasn't for several happy coincidences, my chapter in geo-caching may have never been written.

It was only by chance that a coworker stopped by my office one day with a yellow Garmin eTrex GPS unit in his hands. Being the kind of guy that would ooh and ahh over anything running on a battery, I gleefully snatched the device and ran outside. I watched in awe as the little guy drawn on the screen would move when I moved, and little tracks would appear along the path I traveled. I was in technology heaven!

It wasn't that I was new to GPS. I had used it several times before in rental cars. But now, watching the little guy on the screen follow my movements, I realized that I was holding the same tech-nology in the palm of my hand. With two AA batteries and this device, I could command 24 satellites in space to do my bidding. It was a powerful feeling.

So what did I do with this incredible power? I created a listing service on the Internet to help people locate plastic containers in the woods.

The science fiction writer and scientist Arthur C. Clarke once said that any sufficiently advanced technology is indistinguishable from magic. Although I understand the fundamental concept behind GPS, I am still amazed when I turn it on and within seconds it can pinpoint my location on the planet.

Beyond technology there is also a certain magic in the players, like a shiny star in the eyes of many who go out and find their first cache or their thousandth. The metal box, mint tin, or plastic container becomes a quest for the treasures of the ancients, the holy grail, and the ark of the lost covenant. Every adult and child are wide-eyed and excited about what's hidden behind that stump over the hill.

I've been traveling down the geocaching path for six years now. The geocaching community has helped build the path over the years, but I have been fortunate to have the chance to build the occasional footbridge or stepping stone to guide it along. I'm still honored to be part of the journey. I hope you will find geocaching as enjoyable as I have.

Just make sure to mark the location of your vehicle. This comes from experience.

Jeremy Irish
Founder, Geocaching.com

Introduction

Reading about nature is fine, but if a person walks in
the woods and listens carefully, he can learn more than
what is in books, for they speak with the voice of God.

JOHN WASHINGTON CARVER (1864–1943)

Geocaching has been described, tongue firmly planted in
cheek, as a scavenger hunt that uses multi-million-dollar
satellites to locate worthless toys.

That's certainly one way of looking at it.

There's another way of seeing the hobby, though, and it is that
geocaching brings people closer to nature, closer to each other, and
closer to things that give them joy. It's a hobby that can be practiced
in a myriad of different ways, with varying activities and different
goals, and can support nearly any way of relating to others and the
world.

I should note before I go too far down this particular road that
many people see geocaching as an intensely competitive activity
that pits them against others, against time, and against their own
limitations. They are interested in accumulating statistics, racking
up numbers, and proclaiming themselves king of the hill. They will

plant uninteresting caches for the numbers, ignore guidelines for the numbers, and alienate family and friends for the numbers.

I am not one of these people. If I were, I wouldn't be writing this book.

My spiritual background is eclectic and so too are my beliefs today about humanity and the world around us. Perhaps you have come from a religious upbringing that has allowed you to relate positively to the earth, and if you have, that's wonderful—but in the western world it's also fairly unusual. The Judeo-Christian belief system (on which most of the west's legal systems rest) articulates an understanding that God meant for humanity to dominate (and in some ways subjugate) the earth; and as we move further into a time of clear crisis for the planet we see the tragic results of that kind of thinking.

Mining (and in particular strip mining) destroys habitats and pollutes water supplies; oil drilling has killed countless creatures and permanently injured the environment; the gases we emit in our never-ending search for convenience and ease of lifestyle may be what, ironically enough, will eventually eradicate the very life we're trying to make easier. We kill animals in appallingly cruel ways for food, for clothing, for sport, or simply for the hell of it. We generate enough garbage to bury whole cities. And that's without even going into the idiocy of the weapons systems we have developed to selectively murder certain subsets of our species or the enthusiasm with which we undertake that eradication.

We abuse land because we regard it as a commodity belonging to us. When we see land as a community to which we belong, we may begin to use it with love and respect. (Aldo Leopold)

If I've learned anything as a result of my time spent thus far on the planet, it's that we're in this together. The only way we have any hope of survival is to realize that and start acting like we know it.

We're going to live as a result of the decisions we make and the actions we take, or we're going to die; but there's nothing that we do that has no effect on others. There's a wonderful passage in Norton Juster's *The Phantom Tollbooth* about the world's inter-relatedness:

"You may not see it now," said the Princess of Pure Reason, looking knowingly at Milo's puzzled face, "but whatever we learn has a purpose and whatever we do affects everything and everyone else, if even in the tiniest way. Why, when a housefly flaps his wings, a breeze goes round the world; when a speck of dust falls to the ground, the entire planet weighs a little more; and when you stamp your foot, the earth moves slightly off its course. Whenever you laugh, gladness spreads like the ripples in a pond; and whenever you're sad, no one anywhere can be really happy. And it's much the same thing with knowledge, for whenever you learn something new, the whole world becomes that much richer."

I've come more and more to see the world in this way, as an organic whole, a series of inter-related lives and beings and moments. Nature has its laws, and we disobey them at our peril. And they're not bad laws: the law of consequences of one's actions. It seems we could do worse than apply them to our lives.

But what does all of this have to do with geocaching?

Everything, I think. Geocaching shows us, up close and personal, the impact of humanity's interaction with the physical world (I'll leave the impact of our interaction with the psychic world for another book) and deepens an understanding of and love for everything that surrounds us. And it happens imperceptibly, without one even noticing it: the awareness creeps up and soon one finds oneself saying things like, "I can't believe how much garbage picnickers leave behind!"

It's good for you, this geocaching. Like it or not.

ONE

What Is It All About?

The woods are lovely, dark and deep
But I have promises to keep
And miles to go before I sleep . . .
—ROBERT FROST

My teenaged stepchildren are spending the weekend with us as I write this. They're playing with the family cat, and I can hear them laughingly mocking the words to the *Hokey-Pokey:* "You do the hokey-pokey, and you turn yourself around: that's what it's all about!"

In my worst nightmares, I wonder: is that, indeed, what it's all about?

But it's good place to start in a book about opening your heart through geocaching, because there's a significant knowledge base that you need to at least hear (and perhaps even acquire) before you can decide whether geocaching is, in fact, something you'd like to explore for yourself.

So let's talk about what it is all about.

The Antecedents

Scavenger hunts have been around for many centuries, originally perhaps as a simulation of what was once important and necessary work—the hunt for food. The reenactment has taken on many guises: the Easter egg hunt, hide-and-go-seek, medieval party games. The twentieth century refined the game with the addition of advanced technology and produced the University of Chicago scavenger hunt, the University of Melbourne Scavenger Hunt, the Tricadecathlonomania, the Leif Erikson Hunt, and Snap-Shot City among (many) others.

The most direct antecedent to geocaching is an activity still practiced today called letterboxing. A box or bag is hidden and searchers are given directions with which to find it ("Go to the oak tree on this path, turn right, take three large steps, and look for another oak tree. The hide is there."); the name perhaps remembers a time when letters—and particularly illicit *billets doux*—were hidden in such a manner.

Today, of course, illicit love notes are sent as emails . . . but that, too, is another story for another day.

A Brief History of Geocaching

The GPS (Global Positioning System) is a satellite navigation system developed by the United States Department of Defense and intended for military use by the U.S. and its allies. The system's signals were scrambled (a measure known as selective availability, ostensibly for national security concerns), so that GPS devices used by civilians were only accurate to about three hundred feet, making them essentially useless. Imagine the boater, for example, depending on a GPS receiver to navigate a set of shoals: three hundred feet off is the difference between a safe passage and running aground!

Geocaching officially began in May of 2000, when then-president Bill Clinton announced that the United States government was turning selective availability off for civilian owners of GSP devices. When selective availability was turned off, the accuracy rate of civilian GPS units zoomed up to thirty feet or better; the first person to see and take advantage of the new possibilities offered was an inventor named Dave Ulmer, then active on a Usenet newsgroup.

A mere three days after selective availability was turned off, he outlined a "stash hunt" in which people could post GPS coordinates (called waypoints) on the Internet that would bring one to a "stash" hidden in much the same way as earlier scavenger hunts had hidden their treasures. He followed up his proposal by creating just such a stash:

> —Now that SA is off we can start a worldwide Stash Game!! With Non-SA accuracy is (sic.) should be easy to find someone's stash from waypoint information. Waypoints of secret stashes could be shared on the Internet, people could _navigate to the stashes and get some stuff. The only rule would for stashes is: Get some Stuff, Leave some Stuff!!
> Have Fun!!
> Dave . . .

Within weeks there was a Yahoo! group for geocachers—or "stashers," as they were called at that time. Some concern over the possible negative connotations of the word led one of the Yahoo! group members, Matt Stum, to suggest "geocaching" as an alternative. "Several people have already stated their dislike for the term 'stash' on the basis that it sounds illegal," he wrote on the twentieth of May in 2000. "The word cache both brings forth feelings of nostalgia for the days of exploring, as well as a 'techie' feeling for those that associate it with computer memory." The name stuck, and the hobby was launched. But not by Ulmer. He became disillusioned very early on with what he saw as the potential environmental hazards of sending hundreds of people trampling through underbrush in search of a cache. He left the hobby for a number of years and only returned to it as a serious presence in 2006.

In the meantime, while learning about GPS technology, a Seattle-based entrepreneur named Jeremy Irish came upon the first website devoted to GPS-stashing and immediately imagined an Internet presence that not only explained the game but could be a gathering-place and information exchange for those playing it. By September of 2000, Irish had founded Groundspeak, the company that currently owns and operates the geocaching.com website.

Although there are several companies and organizations that have from time to time attempted to challenge Groundspeak's dominance over the hobby, most have had little or no success for all the same reasons that anyone challenging a monopoly fails. (See Appendix A for other geocaching enterprises.)

So . . . what?

So by now you have a sense at least of what geocaching involves: something hidden, something found, and all by means of a GPS device.

So let's get more specific.

The major geocaching organization, Groundspeak, defines geocaching as "an entertaining adventure game for GPS users. Participating in a cache hunt is a good way to take advantage of the wonderful features and capability of a GPS unit. The basic idea is to have individuals and organizations set up caches all over the world and share the locations of these caches on the Internet. GPS users can then use the location coordinate to find the caches. Once found, the cache may provide the visitor with a wide variety of rewards.

All the visitor is asked to do is if they get something, they should try to leave something for the cache."

Already in this definition you'll be getting a feel for the appeal the activity holds for geeks: "tak(ing) advantage of the wonderful features and capability of a GPS unit." And if you imagine people having endless discussions about which brand of GPS is better than which other, you'd be right. For me, and I'll probably be returning to this theme *ad infinitum, ad nauseam* throughout the book, that part of the definition would read, *it's taking advantage of the wonderful features of the world around us and the capability of other humans to find beauty and meaning in them.*

The neologism "geocaching" can best be understood by breaking it apart: it contains the prefix *geo* (for geography) and the base word *caching* (for the process of hiding/finding a cache). In computer terms, a cache is information stored in memory to make it quick to retrieve, but the term has also been used for many years in hiking and camping circles as a hiding place for concealing and preserving provisions; and of course *caché* is French for hidden (my stepson Jacob placed a cache in a cliff and named it the Hard Rock Caché!).

What's in a cache? First, and perhaps most importantly, every cache contains a logbook to be signed by geocachers who have found the cache. Some people merely scrawl their names; others leave wonderful personal notes, comments on the cache or the location, and/or anecdotes that might be relevant to the cache owner or other geocachers finding it. Jeremy Irish speaks of this in his interview later on: what he likes to leave behind is a detailed account of finding the cache. I love reading logbooks when I find a cache—this has replaced the "treasure hunt" aspect of the hobby for me—and often come across interesting and occasionally endearing entries there.

Caches also contain trinkets of some sort, most often of an age and condition to make an exchange uninteresting—though, as we will see, many caches are themed and well-maintained as to their contents. Caches may also contain what are known as "hitchhikers," objects that travel from cache to cache.

Caches are sometimes found by non-geocachers, known in the jargon (and thanks to the popularity of J. K. Rowling) as "muggles." Because of this, every cache should include a notation of what it is, and why it is there, directing people to the geocaching website for further information.

One cache that was frequently "muggled" (it has since then been archived, and replaced with another that is far less easy to find) was by Lake Massabesic in Auburn, New Hampshire; it was hidden among some rock ledges that afford a wonderful view of the lake, particularly

Every cache contains a logbook.

at sunset. The day I found this cache, it had been very recently muggled (i.e., a non-geocacher had discovered it, and in this case written in the log), and the following note left:

6-9-05
My Sweetheart and I used to come here often.
She died 6-8-05 2:10 A.M. I miss you so very much my cupcakes & I always will.
My love forever and alwayS.
xo xo xo xo xo xo xo xo xo xo xo xo xo xo xo xo xo xo xo xo xo
P.S. may you be at last as happy and fulfilled as you made me feel.
I LOVE YOU BRENDA

I don't generally copy out the notes I find in logbooks, but this one was clearly an exception. I do read back through logbooks (unless the conditions are difficult—I'm not *that* enamored of standing in sleet or high winds or heavy rain in order to satisfy my curiosity!), and one often comes across some lovely notes.

Logbooks are a wonderful way for the cache owner to see how his or her cache has touched others. They also serve as proof that a geocacher did actually find the cache, and for those interested in accumulating numbers, this "find verification" is important. Caches must then also be logged at the geocaching site; geocachers can duplicate their logbook entries here, or perhaps write more, since writing in a logbook is often done in adverse weather or other extreme conditions. The geocaching site keeps one's statistics, and for many people, these are important, whether as a record of where they've been or in playing the numbers game.

Types of Caches

The next thing we need to look at is the cache itself, as there are many kinds of caches, and different people are attracted to doing all, some, or just one of them.

Here, then, are the major sorts of caches you might place or encounter in geocaching:

- **Traditional caches** are the most common and represent what we could call the "basic" cache type. A traditional cache is found via GPS coordinates and is comprised of a waterproof container (locked plastic containers and ammo boxes are the most frequently used), a logbook, and trade items.

- **Multi caches** consist, as their name implies, of multiple cache locations (though there is only generally one cache containing the logbook and trade items). Each location then leads the seeker

Placing an ammo box.

to the next one, either through giving additional GPS coordinates or other instructions.

- **Offset caches** are similar to the multi-cache, except that the initial GPS coordinates take the cacher to a location containing information that encodes the final cache coordinates. An example would be to direct the cacher to a plaque where the digits of a date on the plaque correspond to the coordinates of the final cache containing the logbook; many people, however, would argue that the "take the numbers from a plaque" cache is a puzzle (and not a very good one). An offset or multi usually has the next coordinates written down clearly, often on a laminated strip of paper hidden somewhere, say in a thirty-five-millimeter film canister (remember film canisters?) in the crook of a tree. There is endless discussion as to whether there is in fact such a thing as an offset cache, or if all offsets are in fact merely multi-caches.

- **Mystery/puzzle caches** do not include a listed set of coordinates for the cache. The cacher locates them after solving a puzzle, following clues, and other devices that then lead him or her to the final cache containing the logbook. This should be my favorite cache type, as I devour mystery novels and race the fictional sleuth to the uncovering of the culprit. Many of the puzzle caches, as we will see, do not fit that "mystery" mindset and involve mathematical computations, decrypting codes, and so on. Paul, my husband, is especially well-known in geocaching circles for placing this kind of cache.

- **Micro caches** are, as their name implies, very small caches. They are often placed in film canisters, in the small metal boxes used to conceal keys, or in special-purpose "nano" containers that are about a half an inch tall on all sides. They are most often found in urban areas where a traditional cache container would be impossible to hide.

- **Letterbox hybrids** combine both a geocaching log and a letterbox log in the final cache. Remember the reference to letterboxing in the Short History of Geocaching earlier on in this chapter? There are usually two sets of directions for finding a hybrid cache: The GPS coordinates for geocachers to follow, and letterbox directions for letterboxers to follow. For more on letterboxing, see chapter nine.

- **Virtual caches** are caches without a final physical cache (no box, logbook, or trade items). Instead, the location contains (or is) some other described object or view. When we first moved to Manchester, there was a mural covering an entire side of a building. Titled *Lest We Forget* (you'll grasp the irony of this name in a moment), it pictured scenes from the city's past—the mills, the immigrants, the tremendously hard labor that built Manchester. We wanted to draw people's attention to this incredibly moving display, and so made it a virtual cache, so that it could become a destination and perhaps a way of giving people a sense of the past. The building was subsequently purchased and made into a restaurant, and the mural (amid much protest) painted over because the new owners found it too gaudy for the restaurant's style. We obviously archived this particular virtual cache (more on archiving later), but were glad we'd been able to draw so many people to it before it was destroyed.

How do people show they've been to a virtual cache, as there is no logbook there to sign? Generally geocachers are required to email the cache owner with information that was found at the site (a date, a name on a plaque or a memorial, for example) or to post a picture of themselves at the site with the GPS receiver in hand.

Groundspeak has as of 2006 ended all virtual caches because too many uninteresting caches were being placed. There was an attempt to make a "wow" rule, stating that there must be something interesting at the site, but the subjectiveness of this became an issue and so the ban was put in place.

- **Webcam caches** are similar to virtual caches in that they don't have containers or logbooks; instead, the GPS coordinates point to a location where there is a public webcam, where the geocacher captures his or her image on the webcam for find verification. The same ban has been placed on webcam caches.

- **Event caches** are located at a gathering attended by geocachers. These can be anything from a full day of geocaching in a small defined area with caches placed temporarily for the event date only, to dinners and other socialization opportunities. I co-host three such events every year at a local Irish pub.

- **Cache-In, Trash-Out (CITO) events** are variations on event caches, in which geocachers gather to clean up the trash in a designated area to improve the environment. The expression "cache in, trash out" is a common one in geocaching, and many geocachers routinely carry rubbish bags with them and pick up whatever cans, wrappers, and other refuse they see as they go along in their travels. I have a box of such bags in the trunk of my car and need to replace it with some regularity.

(And I truly cannot think of CITO events without hearing the words of political satirist and songwriter Roy Zimmerman in my head, as he and his "conservative girlfriend" go "wilderness trashing" every weekend. Good thing there are geocachers to clean up after them!)

Why geocache?

The reasons that people geocache are as varied as the people themselves.

Some people just want to get out of the house; some want to get closer to their families, and others want some time *away* from their families; some are nourishing their need for adventure and exploration while others are feeding into their need to compete; some want to be alone in the woods, others want to enjoy a group activity; some want to solve a complex mental challenge, while others want to rest their brains for a while. The comparisons and contrasts could go on forever.

I asked geocachers themselves what they found enriching about geocaching, and received a number of different responses from participants in the forums on the geocaching website:

> For us it enriches our relationship. With school and work it is tough to find time to do things together. So nearly every weekend we take one day and go geocaching. It gives us time away from the everyday stress of the real world and allows us to talk and share our feelings while we are walking to and from the caches. Secondly, once

we had acquired the necessary equipment, geocaching is a cheap endeavor. There is no need to spend money every weekend to go to the movies, go golfing, or to go to sporting events. Therefore it is because of geocaching that my girlfriend and I get to spend quality time together doing something that we both love. *(Bccruiser, Bellingham, Washington)*

Wouldn't be doing it if it weren't. It's a combination of going places, meeting people and everything else. I guess it boils down to having new experiences—and if that's not enriching, nothing is. *(Corp of Discovery, Blue Island, Illinois)*

Two main things, community and going to great places you wouldn't have even bothered to visit even if you had known about them.
(Blue Deuce, Iowa)

I'm sure there are lots of reasons people do this—here are mine. Not very existential, but heartfelt.

1. Exploring places I know about but never bothered go. I won't go exploring without a goal of some type—the cache is a great goal.

2. Discovering nice spots that I didn't know about—I almost squeal with pleasure when I make a great find that I would not have without the goal of a cache.

3. I think many, if not all of us are collectors at heart. Caches/finds are a great thing to collect and get you outdoors and off the couch.

4. My nine-year-old daughter is starting to like caching. I'm hoping we'll continue to share some nice time together caching when she's to old to otherwise want to hang with dad.

5. I love getting outdoors and hiking in the woods. Again, probably wouldn't do it without some goal.

(MuchAdo, Manchester, New Hampshire)

I geocache with my twin seven-year-old boys and occasionally my wife. I use it as a motivator to get the kids to do their homework. "If you finish your homework, we'll go geocaching after I get home from work." It allows me to unwind after a hard day at work and to spend some quality time with my family. Not sitting in front of a TV.

However, I think the biggest enrichment is the sense of team/family we get of going out and finding these as a family. *(Chonk, Kentwood, Michigan)*

I walk around in the woods a lot and a lot of the time it has no purpose, just to walk around and look at what is going on around you. But with geocaching it gives you a purpose to walk and wonder— you are looking for something out there and not just wandering around lost. *(Nomad85, Ivoryton, Connecticut)*

Jeannette and Geocaching

My own experience has been serendipitous.

I'm married to a confirmed gadget person, and one Christmas I thought to buy Paul a handheld GPS unit. He had been using GPS technology on the sailboat on which he races, and had spoken in glowing terms of the receiver (I myself crossed the Atlantic— twice—in a sailboat, navigating only by sextant, so I could certainly appreciate his enthusiasm). He unwrapped the gift certificate with delight—I don't trust myself to actually *select* the electronic gadgets in question—and exclaimed, "Cool, now I can go geocaching!"

I had never heard of it.

I also considered myself too busy to incorporate a new activity into my repertoire (this was supposed to be a toy for Paul, not me, after all), but once again—as happens often enough that I really *should* consider listening—the Universe was prodding me to go where I needed to be. The old expression of "going with the flow" is so relevant to all of us: accept change, try new things (especially when they are just lying there in the path in front of you, ready to be picked up!), see what happens. Paul really *really* wanted me to try it with him. So—with nothing that could be said to be even approaching good grace—I went. Once, I said.

We started geocaching, first the two of us, then including his children on the weekends they were *chez* Cézanne. And an odd thing happened to me.

I had been saddened by our recent plan to move from Cambridge, Massachusetts, to the queen city of Manchester in southern New Hampshire. It's less than sixty miles away—but every one of those miles is heading inland. I'd lived for a very long time near the ocean and wasn't able to imagine myself anywhere else; but now I was abruptly thrust outdoors, exploring lakes and streams and hills and woods—especially the woods—and I suddenly realized that I wasn't missing the ocean as much anymore.

I wasn't missing the ocean anymore—instead, I was seeing it as part of an organic whole: part of nature. And I realized that by restricting my love to just one part of what the earth has to offer, I had been cutting myself off from experiences that were equally enriching and often breathtaking.

> Only when the last tree has died, and the last river has been poisoned, and the last fish has been caught, will we realize that we can't eat money. (Cree Proverb)

Would I have gone into the woods had it not been for geocaching? I don't particularly like admitting it, but the answer is probably not.

I had loved visiting Walden Pond in Concord long before I geocached, of course; I walked around it in all sorts of weather, watched hawks, listened to the trains rumbling by, imagined Thoreau finding solitude there. But I never made the connection—I never realized it was the *woods per se* that were drawing me. I thought, with my then-usual cerebral approach, that it was in fact the association with a past literary giant that made me feel connected when I was there.

I was wrong.

And I probably would never have gone into New Hampshire's woods if it were not for geocaching. I would certainly not have seen what I have seen, as the necessity of following someone else's directions taking one, most often, to a spot that the cache-hider loves, would not have been there to guide me. There are remote places near the city I would never have dreamed were there, and hidden scenes of breathtaking beauty I would never have guessed were over that hill or down that trail.

I've come upon abandoned buildings and built lives in my head for the people who once lived there. I've found old farmhouse wells deep in the woods and seen a peregrine falcon's nest on the side of a tall city building. And I'm always eager, now, to grab my hiking boots and my stick and head out whenever my husband or stepchildren want to go, because I know that I'll come back refreshed . . . and, sometimes, amazed.

Grab my hiking boots and a stick.

Because of geocaching, I finally came to understand James Fenimore Cooper's words in *The Pathfinder:* "Look about you and judge for yourself. I'm in church now; I eat in church, drink in church, sleep in church. The earth is the temple of the Lord, and I wait on him hourly, daily, without ceasing, I humbly hope."

A Conversation with Mary Votava

Mary Votava is one of the stars of the Sci-Fi channel reality show *Who Wants to be a Superhero?* Her character, Monkey Woman, is a "comedic comedy superhero character" that Mary herself created. Her website notes that "Mary is determined to make it in the TV / film industry and is currently occupied with this endeavor, and supporting a life that allows the for the flexibility and persistence required to succeed. Most of her time is now spent schlepping her tail around Los Angeles to get to auditions, attending acting classes, figuring out new and old ways to meet casting directors, and even occasionally practicing her art."

Why do you geocache?

Geocaching is like a mini treasure hunt. I have always enjoyed adventure, puzzles, etc. Growing up, my dad used to make *Da Vinci Code*-esque quests for my siblings and me, and Easter egg hunts were one of the highlights of my year. Also, I love the outdoors and hiking. Getting to combine two of my favorite activities makes for, in my opinion, the perfect hobby.

What is your style of caching . . . how do you "play the game?"

At first, I was just competing to stay ahead of my best friend,

"PirateKing," both in numbers and FTFs. *(FTF refers to first-to-find, explained in detail in the glossary.)* But I got a little obsessed in those first couple months and had to take it down a notch when I would find myself racing across town in the middle of the night, in the rain, with the flu, just to be FTF on an Altoids tin. I practice moderation now, and will take a day or half day now and then to go do some caching, or if I'm going somewhere and have an extra hour or two to kill I might grab a few in the area.

What is the most moving or magical thing that has happened to you when geocaching? Can you share that experience?

I've had some *very* memorable experiences geocaching and am good about putting any fun stories in my logs. Perhaps one of the most magical stories relates to my recent appearance on *Who Wants to be a Superhero?*—the evening before I had my audition for the show, I had *just* finished sewing my costume (with my mom's help) when I noticed an email notification on my computer for a newly published cache about five miles away. I hadn't gone after an FTF for a while, and decided to reward myself for my hard work by going after this one. It also happened to be my two hundredth cache, so it was a bit of a landmark. My mom and I jumped in my car and tore off towards the coordinates, armed with flashlights and my Geko. We found the cache, and were FTF, but the best part was that the first thing I saw when I opened the cache was a monkey beanie baby. "It's a sign!" I told my mom . . . and it was! I took that little monkey with me to the superhero "lair" and had it on my bed there the whole time we were filming.

Another fun memory was the time I fell on a cactus while geo-caching. It's such a classic blunder, but how many people can say they've *actually* fallen on a cactus?

Do you experience geocaching as being part of a community? If so, in what way(s)? Have people from the community become your friends?

Being in the geocaching community almost feels like being a member of a secret society or something. Because it's not yet a widely known hobby, finding other people who know about it and share a passion for geocaching is a sort of instant bond. We are privy to secret stashes all over the planet. We understand the necessity to paw around under newspaper stands, crawl through bushes, investigate tidy piles of rocks, and dismantle public fixtures. We know the real meaning of the word "muggle." I've met some wonderful friends through geocaching who I am truly blessed to have in my life!

What sorts of things do you pick up? What do you leave behind?

I pretty much only collect people's signature items now. I used to take and leave small trade items, and still do on occasion if I see something I like (such as a stuffed monkey). Sometimes I'll find an item in a cache that's on my shopping list, which is nice. I mostly leave my signature item now: a plastic capsule with a Fimo frog inside. (I name them all individually . . . the most recent batch were the "British Monarchs" frogs: Henry, William, Elizabeth, Aethelrud, etc.). When I started making the frogs (in honor of Signal), I had no idea I'd become known for "Monkey Woman" or I would've gone with a monkey theme instead. I'll probably switch at some point. I'm no sculptor so the frogs are a hassle to make.

How do you feel when you geocache?

I feel like a little kid again, excited and mischievous, when I'm geocaching. I almost always have some little adventure or fun happenstance; very few of my logs just say TNLNSL (took nothing, left nothing, signed log).

What question am I forgetting to ask that you'd like to answer?

One of the unexpected perks I've found about geocaching is that it makes me "stop to smell the roses." People tend to plant caches at public attractions, and there are myriad cool little parks, niches, and monuments all around the community that I would never have known about had I not come to them in pursuit of a cache.

TWO

Finders, Keepers

If ever you come upon a grove of ancient trees which have
grown to an exceptional height, shutting out a view of sky by
a veil of pleached and intertwining branches, then the loftiness
of the forest, the seclusion of the spot and your marvel at the
thick unbroken shade in the midst of the open spaces,
will prove to you the presence of deity.

—LUCIUS ANNAEUS SENECA (5 B.C.E.–65 C.E.)

Let's talk about finding caches. That's the essence of the hobby for most people, after all: going out and finding a cache, with whatever happens to be inside it.

Whatever happens to be inside it varies. As noted before, every cache must contain a logbook. This is generally a small notebook, as traditional caches in plastic containers or ammo cans have plenty of space; it's usually in a sealed plastic bag along with pens and pencils with which the geocacher can write. Micro caches contain smaller logbooks, usually consisting of folded waterproof paper (or even tiny rolls of paper that you need tweezers to extract!); obviously, these cache "logbooks" do not allow for long entries, which are recorded instead on the geocaching site.

Finding a cache is an equally powerful experience, as you are opening yourself up to being touched by the part of someone else that they have placed "out there." We make very deliberate choices about the things we allow the world to see and experience of ourselves. We think about how we present ourselves to the world: we choose clothing, makeup, hairstyles. We have our bodies pierced and tattooed; we follow (or don't follow) fashions; we drive cars that project an image of who we are. We choose professions, activities, and even partners based on the measure that we allow others to see us—or that we choose to reveal ourselves to them.

So perhaps in a smaller but more intense way, we choose what we place in caches. We make them into memorials or museums; but we do it all deliberately.

And sometimes we don't stop to think that it works both ways.

What does someone else's cache say to you? How does it present the person who placed it? What does it tell you about that person? Is this someone you want to know better, or perhaps not at all?

Can you pause for a moment and be grateful for what the person was willing to share about himself or herself?

Getting Started

How do you find a cache?

Your first step is to buy or borrow a handheld GPS unit. This is *not* the same thing as the GPS navigation systems available on many cars, and that's all that I'm going to say about the devices themselves. For now, we're going to assume that you have one in hand. Literally.

Your next step is to your computer, where you'll access geocaching.com. This is the community, the gathering-place, the Information Central of geocaching. Basic membership is free, so go ahead and create an account.

As with all other online accounts, people create interesting names for themselves on the geocaching site. I chose Angevine because I grew up in Angers, France, and a female who comes from that region is known as an *angevine* (for those of you not fluent in French and curious, a *male* from Angers is an *angevin*). My husband is NotThePainter—to distinguish him from that *other* Paul Cézanne! Find a name that you'll feel comfortable being called by at geo-events . . . and that you won't mind scrawling in a logbook in a high wind on a cold December morning somewhere.

Step two of the registration process will ask you where you're located, down to listing your home GPS coordinates (if you don't know them yet, that's fine, this page is optional) and the units of measurement (Imperial or metric) you want to see displayed when looking up caches. At the bottom of this page is the option to check a box asking that Groundspeak send you a weekly email listing new caches in your area. If you're not interested in being "first to find," this is a *great* way to keep up with caches that might be easy for you to access.

Step three allows you to enter personal information about your-self that will be available to others accessing the geocaching site, so determine how much you want to share with the community at large.

At this point you'll probably want to click the "Getting Started" option in the menu on the left side of your screen. This takes you to a page filled with wonderful links that you'll want to spend some time reading: geocaching resources (geocaching frequently asked questions, a history of geocaching, geocaching in the news, and Groundspeak support); geocaching events, complete with an event calendar; geocaching services with information on geo-teaming (teambuilding events that involve geocaching); and the important geocaching guides.

The guides are really essential for you to read before you begin.

They're clear, well written, and complete, and will give you all the information you need, all in one place. Some of the information in the guides is similar to what you'll read here, but it doesn't hurt to absorb the information from more than one source. It's been said that one must learn—and forget—something three times before one has really learned it, and it seems to me that a good way to do that is by listening to many different voices speaking about the subject one wishes to learn.

So read the geocaching guides! They include:

- Guide to Finding a Geocache

- Guide to Hiding a Geocache

- Guide to Buying a GPS unit for Geocaching

- Geocaching Listing Guidelines

- Geocaching.com Glossary

Once you've done all this, you're pretty much ready to get started. I expect that you want to go out there and find something, right? So let's do it.

Getting Ready

Alas, we're not in the woods yet.

And for some very good reasons. Jackson Browne spoke in *After the Deluge* of people being "confused" by the "magnitude of her fury." That's nature that he's talking about, and the old advertising tagline is relevant here: it's not only not nice to fool (with) Mother Nature, it can be deadly.

For you, that is. Nature doesn't care. As mentioned in the introduction, nature has neither rewards nor punishments—what nature has are *consequences*. And the consequences aren't like those we give our children, where there can be leeway, mitigating circumstances, a second chance. You mess up out there and you can die. No take-backs, no second chances. It really is that simple.

So be very clear about where you are going and what you need to do to get there—and back—safely.

The geocaching site recommends that you not go into remote areas alone. This is good advice, though I will confess that I have not always taken it, as I am often happiest when I'm by myself and have the space and time to really appreciate my surroundings, to sit with them, to meditate in them. Perhaps you, too, like solitude; but if you're not accustomed to going into the woods alone, try it first with a companion. You might find that you'd prefer to keep your solitude for more accessible venues.

Whatever you decide to do, make sure that someone knows where you're going (and that means *exactly* where you're going—"Bear Brook State Park" isn't enough), and check in with that person when you return. Mobile telephones do not work in remote locations, so do not depend on your cell to summon help. If you do want to go geocaching alone, consider taking a ham radio course and buying a handheld ham radio transmitter. No matter how outdoor-savvy you think you are, accidents can happen to anyone.

Bring water. There's an old wives' tale—the rural equivalent of an urban legend—that running water is drinkable water. It isn't. You have no idea what is upstream, what pollutants are in that seemingly clear stream, or how any of it might affect you. There are backpacks available that include a reservoir of water (with easy access to it through a drinking tube), or you can fill and carry water bottles—your choice, but bring water. It's easy to get dehydrated, and by the time you feel thirsty, it's already happened.

(A bit of homespun wisdom gleaned from a member of the Sports Car Club of America, comprised of people who are used to being outdoors for long stretches of time: Drink until your urine is almost clear, and then drink some more. That's the only way to be sure that you're getting enough hydration when you're out there.)

Bring energy bars, trail mix, or dried fruit, too: you may feel just fine when you set out, but hunger can take you by surprise, make you feel light-headed and even ill. Be prepared with more than you think you'll need. Avoid candy bars and anything sweet: the sugar high feels just fine, but you don't want to crash when you still need some reserves of strength.

If you are going into the woods, and it is hunting season, wear blaze orange. In fact, find out what your local regulations are before you go out: some require that you wear specific clothing. Outdoor-sports stores usually carry orange vests you can slip on over whatever outerwear you have; but be careful—once you put your backpack on, you're essentially no longer wearing it when seen from the rear.

Orange woolen hats may not be a stunning fashion choice, but keep in mind that your first and most important goal when you go into the woods is that you want to come out of them again. It's a myth that hunters will mistake you for a deer; the issue is, rather, that you may be somewhere *behind* the animal at which they're aiming, and the bullet will thereby follow the sightline and find you as well. So make sure you're visible from as great a distance as possible.

Don't depend solely on your GPS receiver to get you in and out of anywhere. Batteries fail; devices are dropped and broken. Bring a compass (I have one embedded in the top of my walking-stick)—but take the time first to learn to use it. Pay attention to what is around you: trail markings, trees, anything that can act as a landmark. You don't have Ariadne's thread to help you out, and anywhere that you're lost can feel very much like a labyrinth indeed.

Perhaps too obvious to mention (but I'll mention them anyway) are your organic or chemical companions: sunscreen and bug spray.

Not having either can make your geocaching experience extremely unpleasant. Also bring a small first-aid kit, either one you purchased (I carry one meant to go on a small boat, for example) or one that you put together. Always bring a knife of some sort and a whistle.

Be prepared for inclement weather. An all-weather hat may be a better choice than a baseball cap; bringing a light fold-up poncho in your backpack is another option. In the fall and winter months I always slip a chemical hand-warmer into my backpack, just in case; I also always have a so-called "astronaut's" blanket folded there. It adds practically no weight or bulk and could very well save your life if you are hurt and stranded somewhere.

Invest if you can in good footwear. What you buy depends on the level of geocaching you want to do. Most into-the-woods-but-not-scaling-rock-cliffs geocachers find that a pair of hiking shoes or boots works well. Do not buy them and immediately set off on a ten-mile walk; break them in gently and gradually and only go geocaching when they're comfortable. Wear wool socks and bring an extra pair in your backpack; I don't know any geocacher who has not gotten her feet wet at some point, and dry socks are one of life's more comforting pleasures.

A lot of people find that sticks or staffs are useful geocaching tools, even beyond their conventional use as aids to hiking. There are times when the search for a cache involves poking in a hole, under a log, in a stump—in other words, in places where you might not wish to blindly stick your hand. Your staff is then your friend. Geocaching in the winter in snowy places also quickly shows the value of a staff that can clear away snow or "feel" places where, again, you don't want to use your arm.

Later in the book there's a conversation with Jerry Carter, who creates wonderful geocaching staffs. I have one of his and—as the advertising saying goes—I don't leave home without it. But you can just as easily find a wonderful stout stick in the wild, which is what Paul and my stepchildren all did.

You might want to bring some trinkets for exchange when you get to the cache. There is a great deal of discussion about trade items on the geocaching forums, with many people expressing frustration over what they find in caches—usually the kinds of toys one receives in a fast-food restaurant as part of a kid's meal, or, worse, those same toys, only broken. For reasons beyond my understanding, golf balls are also a typical find in a cache. After a while, you'll decide whether the trinket exchange is important to you or not; but always have something nice with you, just in case. The conventional wisdom is to trade up—leave something nicer than what you took. Many geocachers develop signature items, trinkets that they buy or make en masse and place in every geocache they visit; Mary Votava spoke of a signature item she creates to leave in caches in her conversation found between the first and second chapters of this book.

Finally, spend some time with maps. The better you can read a map, the more you'll enjoy and feel proficient at geocaching. Topographical maps are the best; while each geocache includes a terrain rating, these ratings can be subjective and your idea of a tough climb may be very different from mine. You can get online topo maps at topozone.com, which you access by following the link on the cache page: learn to read them and pay special attention to elevation and bodies of water.

And that brings us to the next word of warning . . .

Sometimes 800 feet isn't 800 feet

Your GPS receiver will tell you how far you are from a waypoint or from a cache. What your GPS receiver will *not* take into account is what the terrain looks like between here and there. It might be telling you blithely to proceed forward as you stand, disconsolate, at the edge of a nasty-looking swamp.

GPS devices don't know about nasty-looking swamps.

Which is why you always need to be prepared to walk further than you thought you would, go bushwhacking, skirt bodies of water, and generally do all sorts of things you hadn't initially imagined doing. Allow more time than you think a cache will take, and really consider spending time with the topo maps before you go. By plotting the cache location on the maps, you may be able to avoid some of the nastiness (friends once found out that a cache they were going to seek was actually located on an island in a lake—something better to know *before* one gets there!).

You'll see many wonderful things out there, but keep your eyes out also for the things that aren't as wonderful: logs, holes, and wildlife that does not appreciate your presence. In some areas— New England, where I live, is one of them—the accepted wisdom is

Sighted by a bear

this: if you have ever been out geocaching, you have been sighted by a bear. Generally they will be content with the sighting and amble away without alerting you to their presence, but be aware that the opposite may be true from time to time and you really, *really* don't want to test theories abut what makes bears not want to eat you. Keeping your eyes open and your wits about you—as opposed to trudging down trails with your eyes fixed on your GPS—is a good way to avoid any needless close encounters as well as really take in the beauty that is probably surrounding you.

Remember also that although GPS coordinates are good, they're not perfect. You often need to take several readings and be patient; and the cache hider may not have been thoughtful enough to take and average a number of readings. Heavy tree cover, clouds, and other things can disrupt your unit's ability to narrow down "ground zero" for you (remember that the GPS needs to be in communication with several satellites—at least four, but more is always better—in order to get an accurate reading), older GPS receivers often lose signal under these conditions, and, in addition, many cache hiders don't want to make things too easy for you!

In some ways, the hunt really begins once your GPS announces that you're there.

Once you've been geocaching for a while, you'll start noticing that certain hiders' caches have some consistent characteristics. In some areas, there are cachers whose goal appears to be to place as many caches as they can, without giving much thought to disguising them or making them difficult—they have their own numbers game. When people set out to find this kind of cache, they know the enterprise will be a quick and straightforward proposition.

Paul, as an example of another kind of cacher, has earned a reputation for placing devious caches, and one knows when hunting one of his to look everywhere *but* where one expects a cache to be, including suspended in the air above one's head.

Some hiders are not as subtle. In nearly every area there is what my friend Hans Heilman calls a UPS—an unusual pile of sticks, placed together in a manner that nature never intended. Your search will be quick and fruitful if the cacher has thoughtfully provided you with a UPS!

Most hiders, though, do try to make finding their caches a bit of a challenge, and in some ways the hunt really begins as you move in ever-widening circles, looking around and asking yourself where *you'd* place a cache at these coordinates.

Urban caches present their own particular challenge, as they are generally micros—and there is no end to the attention you'll draw as you hunt around a public bench or signpost! (For this reason, caches are prohibited from being in close proximity to schools, infrastructure—bridges, etc., and government offices. In the post-September 11 United States, one can very quickly find oneself in very unpleasant and possibly secret circumstances if one behaves in too mysterious a manner.)

TNLN (SL)

So you've found the cache. *Youpie!*

Sign the logbook, including any anecdotes abut finding the cache. You can be as descriptive as you want to here; later, when you log your find online, you'll want to be careful not to include any comments that will give away the cache's location. Check out the cache's contents, look for any hitchhikers (see chapter six—Don't Bug Me!—for more about hitchhikers), make an exchange if you'd like. One of the acronyms used widely in the hobby is TNLN: took nothing, left nothing. If you do make an exchange, note in the logbook what you took and what you left.

Be sure to replace the cache where you found it, and to disguise it as much as possible—without leaving behind a telltale stack of sticks!

When you're back home, log your find online by signing on to our account and clicking the link to log a cache. Say as much as you like here—cache owners love to know how their cache placement has touched your life—but be sure not to give away any clues as to its specific location. Take full advantage of this opportunity to share something from your heart: even the most jaded can find ways of opening their hearts when your words lead them there.

Taking it on the Road

I've not yet seen it called geo-tourism, but it ought to be.

This was, it has to be said, a tremendous learning experience for me. After we'd been geocaching a few months, we planned a long weekend trip to Vermont, and Paul immediately began looking up possible caches at our destination as well as along the way.

I won't lie to you, and the truth is easily discovered on the geocaching.com site: I'm not the world's most aggressive geocacher. I don't run out and try to obtain a first-to-find. I often forget about logging my caches altogether. As I've mentioned before, geocaching is for me very much the means to an end: a destination where the journey is infinitely more important.

So when Paul began printing out possible caches, I was annoyed. "We're going up there to enjoy the place, not to *do* something that you can do down here!"

He shrugged. "Let's play it by ear," he said reasonably. "If we don't do them, we don't. If we feel like it, I've got the information."

Ha, I thought, *I know what's going to happen.*

I had no idea what was going to happen.

We went, and by the end of the second day we had pretty much exhausted the tourist activities available. We'd watched glass-blowing at the Simon Pearce factory and seen hot-air balloons at Queechee and we'd walked around Woodstock and visited its art galleries. We'd revisited Cornish, on the New Hampshire side of the Connecticut River, where I once lived and of which I have vibrant, vivid memories. We'd even poked around a museum or two.

Over lunch at Bentley's, Paul pulled out his printouts from the geocaching.com site. "What do you think?"

What I was thinking was that we hadn't planned this trip particularly well. "Okay," I said, with a marked lack of enthusiasm.

So it came to pass that after doing the things that everyone who goes to Vermont does, we ended up doing the things that nobody does except the people who live there. And having a truly wonderful time.

My friend Shel Horowitz has written a book about having fun on a frugal budget, and he suggests that the things one does when being frugal are often more enriching than the things one would do if one had access to limitless funds. By way of example, he compares traveling abroad and staying in impersonal luxury hotels versus staying in exchange situations where one becomes part of the life of the family with which one stays. In which situation, he challenges people, will one learn more about the culture of the country one visits, what people eat, what they like to do?

Geocaching provides a similar conduit for discovery.

I spend quite a lot of my time on Massachusetts' Cape Cod: a week in Falmouth with my family every July; two months in the winter in Provincetown; often, in addition, two weeks on a writing residency in a dune shack. And at all of those venues I walk a lot, explore a lot, think a lot. I'd have said that I know the Cape pretty well.

But geocaching took me down lanes that seemed to be going nowhere and opened up onto vistas where I saw marsh hawks and herons; it led me up hills and onto islands I never saw were connected to the mainland. Geocaching gave me the push it took to walk out to the lighthouse I see every day from my Provincetown apartment, and enabled me to touch—and mourn the death of—a beached dolphin.

Geocaching leads you to the secret places, the hidden places, the magical places. Imagine it: Someone once stood on this very spot and thought, "This is so wonderful I must share it with others!" That's a gift that is from the heart, and it should be part of opening yours. Open yourself to that person's gift, this gift of place and of space, and see what happens. You may be surprised.

Go where tourists don't go. Remember that people generally put caches in special places; take the opportunity to explore those places that they hold special that are far from your home. Open your heart to seeing something new, something different, something that will make you think and feel and be.

And when someone like Paul suggests that you try something different, try it. The Universe puts these opportunities and experiences in front of us every day; we can choose to accept them or to let them pass us by.

I've never regretted one I accepted, though I've regretted a great many that I allowed to pass by.

Be flexible. Be open. Embrace that which is different, challenging. You'll be amazed at how it can change your attitude, your feelings, and your whole being

INTERLUDE

A Conversation
with Jon Stanley

Jon Stanley, also known by his geocaching name of Moun10Bike, is the originator of the geocoin. Some coins are trackable on geocaching.com, some are not; some have their own icons, some do not. There are probably millions of them out there by now.

Jon is a Washington state native, born and raised in Spokane. After receiving a degree in biology and chemistry at Santa Clara University in California, he returned to his home state to pursue a doctorate in genetics at the University of Washington.

He changed his mind after a couple of years in the program and decided to instead pursue his longtime interest in computers, and now works as the test lead for scenery on Microsoft simulations, a job that also allows him to further explore his interests in geography and mapping. It also led him to recently complete a certificate program in Geographic Information Systems (GIS) through Penn State's World Campus.

Jon and his wife, Shauna, have a two-year-old boy, Jameson, who goes by Moun10Tyke.

Why do you geocache?

The activity blends a large number of things of interest to me. I have been a map aficionado all of my life and received a GPS receiver for Christmas in 1995. I used it to map out mountain bike trails in my area (Washington and North Idaho). Mapping out cache routes and expeditions is a big attraction for me. In addition, I work in the computer industry since I have a passion for technology and gadgets, and geocaching is of course strongly tied to that as well. Thirdly, as a lifelong outdoors-oriented person, the hobby appeals to that part of my personality. In short, geocaching combines a number of my strongest interests into one neat package.

What is your style of caching . . . how do you "play the game?"

Hikes are my primary interest. I have very few city hides; most of mine are out in the woods at or near some attraction—a mountain peak, a waterfall, a piece of history, etc. I find caches using various motivations (trying to find the oldest caches in my area, clearing out the closest caches to work and home, etc.), but getting out into the wilderness is my main objective.

What is the most moving or magical thing that has happened to you when geocaching? Can you share that experience?

The most moving and magical things I have experienced have been extremely selfless acts by two individuals. One is actually a string of things done by a local cacher that includes taking a group of us to Alaska at his own expense (he works for Alaska Airlines and was able to fly us free) and "rescuing" one of my geocoins off of eBay by buying it and "trying to send it to me secretively. (As background to explain this, I am the "inventor" of geocoins and created the first ones, so mine have become highly desired among collectors. This leads some ethically challenged people to try auctioning my coins off for money.) Another individual who lives in Europe did a similar thing by purchasing one of my coins off of eBay and sending it to me with no prompting from me. In both cases, I was blown away by these kind acts.

[*There is another point of view that can be taken on the subject of geocoins, or indeed anything that one puts "out there," be it a* cache, a hitchhiker, or any other geo-thing: once it's gone, it's gone. You cannot control what others do—one of life's more difficult lessons to learn!—and you need to assume that some people will not follow the rules you want them to follow, or even know about these rules. It's not entirely fair, perhaps, to describe these people as ethically challenged.]

Do you experience geocaching as being part of a community? If so, in what way(s)? Have people from the community become your friends?

Definitely! My answer to the above question answers that somewhat, but I also have made numerous very good friends through geocaching. I tell my wife, whom I married in 2001 just as geocaching was first starting to take off, that our wedding guest list would look much different if we were getting married today!

What sorts of things do you pick up? What do you leave behind?

I rarely trade anymore, but when I do, I am usually picking up a signature item that I have not seen in a cache before. I leave my own signature items, personalized pins, in all caches that can accommodate them, and in extra-special caches I leave my geocoins.

How do you feel when you geocache?

Alive!

THREE

Hiders, Seekers

I like to take the time out to listen to the trees, much in the same
way that I listen to a seashell, holding my ear against the
rough bark of the trunk, hearing the inner singing of the sap.
It's a lovely sound, the beating of the heart of the tree.

MADELINE L'ENGLE (1918–)

For some people, hiding a cache is even more exciting than
finding one. I happen to be one of those people: I love the
walks in the woods, the discoveries on the trail, the exploration,
and the exhilaration of discovery . . . but I *really* love to place a
cache, I really love to see people's responses to my caches, and I
really love doing the research that is involved in a cache placement.
I've only placed two (can you tell that I'm not particularly interested in numbers?), since they take a great deal of thought and
effort, but I'm very pleased with the ones I have.

I am currently working on a third multi that will take geocachers
on a tour of the "lost places" of Manchester—a sort of tour of what
isn't there anymore. Yeah, I know, that concept *does* present some
intrinsic challenges ("how do you go someplace that isn't there?"
asked my stepdaughter Anastasia): I'm working on them. This is

the sort of consideration that indicates why I don't place a whole lot of caches.

I've included both of my current caches in the appendices to show what a cache can look like; the *Dark Satanic Mills* cache further illustrates the use of waypoints. I placed *Like It Or Not* while I was still spending a great deal of my time in Cambridge, and will probably eventually archive it. In general, cache hiders are responsible for the maintenance of their caches, and caches that are located a long way from one's home are rarely approved. Once we move to Montréal, Paul and I will no doubt archive all of our local caches (unless someone from the area volunteers to take ownership of them from us, a practice known as *adopting* a cache) and start all over again placing caches in Québec.

Where in the World . . .?

Geocaches can be placed in so many different places that the list alone could fill a book. What some people—myself included—enjoy doing is sharing a place that they have found to be special in some way: beautiful, magical, surprising, interesting, inspirational . . . there is no end to the possibilities of sharing, of opening one's heart and one's favorite places to others.

Despite what you might have seen on an unfortunate episode of *Law and Order: Criminal Intent,* caches are *never* buried. You must never put a cache anywhere where it is necessary to dig for it, to displace anything permanently, or to disfigure the environment.

Caches, like cachers themselves, are meant to walk lightly on the earth.

Themed Caches

Some caches have themes: one geocacher in Georgia filled a cache with dog-related items in memory of her recently deceased canine friend; there are book caches, DVD caches, caches that are pure fun (one of my favorites is in Cambridge, Massachusetts; it's called Mutton Box and features sheep trinkets: "Have a mutton? Leave a mutton. Need a mutton? Take a mutton."), caches that reflect obsessions, caches that speak of their creators' dreams, fantasies, flights of fancy.

When a police officer was killed in Manchester, a memorial cache was placed in his favorite park.

In Pennsylvania, one geocacher maintains a holiday cache with a theme that changes four times a year: Halloween, Christmas/Sparkle Season, Valentine's Day/St. Patrick's Day, and finally a patriotic theme. Foreign and special coin caches can be found from Arizona to Maine, though unfortunately they are often, as the expression goes, *muggled,* and the coins taken. There are caches filled with matchbox cars, stuffed animals, board games, keychains.

The limits are your imagination—well, your imagination and the geocaching guidelines, which prohibit placing food of any kind, any sort of scented object (animals will try to access smells), and commercial content (this isn't an advertising forum) in a geocache.

Placing a themed cache means placing something of yourself "out there," whether it's in the wild or in an urban area. It means sharing something that is important to you with the Universe, and amazing things will come back to you, things that will show that the piece of yourself out there has touched others, has been passed along.

Like it Or Not

Paul had already placed three caches of his own, two of which involved intense mathematical calculations, when I decided to get more involved.

In my own way, of course.

I placed a cache in an urban area (Cambridge, Massachusetts) that I almost facetiously called *Like It Or Not.* The goal, as I pointed out in the online cache description, was to get participants to read some poetry—like it or not.

I asked participants to first locate the gravestone of a well-known poet; information obtained there led in turn to his home, his statue, and eventually to the cache itself, in which were three questions forcing the person to look up several poems as well as indicate some personal preferences within the poet's body of work.

My husband helped me place the cache, smiled indulgently, and warned me to not be surprised if no one visited the it. "We're geeks," he said. "Geeks don't read poetry."

I'll admit that traffic to the cache was light and slow, but "puzzle" caches such as this one don't attract the same people who like to tramp through woods and climb cliffs.

But it soon became clear that some geeks, at least, have poetic souls. One of the first people to find the cache works at MIT, which surely says something about a possible relationship between geeks and poetry. Her log reads:

> I thought getting a first-to-find would take months or years of geo-caching experience, but Dave and I saw this posted today and jumped at the opportunity to bike around Cambridge on a beautiful day and find our first FTF.
>
> Really great cache. It was a lot of fun and very informative. Although seeing it through to completion takes conviction, it is well worth it. You might even learn something; we did. Thanks for the cache.

I won't say that the finds poured in after that, not exactly, but each one was more exciting than the last.

For me, reading the cache logs was one of the greatest delights I could imagine. I've spent a fair amount of my life sharing words with others, through my own writing, through teaching, through trying to communicate my delight in poetic expressions to anyone who will listen. I once made my husband and stepchildren stay still through my dramatic reading of Carl Sandberg's brilliant and powerful poem *Chicago*, holding dinner hostage until they had heard the whole thing—and commented upon it.

So there is a little of the dominatrix in me, after all.

And this was not dissimilar: if people wanted to log my cache, they would have to read and reflect on some poetry. I anticipated some annoyed responses. What I didn't expect was such an outpouring of joy, the excitement of having touched someone else through the poet's words.

I really enjoyed working through your cache. After reading the logsheet, I have been reading Longfellow, sharing poetry over the telephone with my daughter, and have encouraged others to do the cache.

This cache will definitely make my 2005 favorites list. Thanks for this very creative and fun cache.

I had reached the head-scratching stage when he made the discovery, fine work pushing the envelope of "hidden in plain sight." Thanks again for taking the time and effort to place this well-crafted cache adventure for my pleasure!

There are lots of geocaches that, after you've finished, you're glad you attempted, but there aren't many about which you can say "I'm really glad I didn't miss that one." This is one of those.

Extremely clever hide that almost defeated me. I have some homework to do before I can officially log this a find. Thanks for the hide. Edit: Received permission to log. I found it refreshing to be "forced" to read some poetry, something I wouldn't have done today without a nudge from Angevine. Thanks again!

Like it or not I did delve into these famous works to solve this cache. Once again, an experience that geocaching help facilitate. Thanks.

Returned with Flying Needle today to explore Wpt. (waypoint) 1. She worked through all the stages to the final, as I watched. I hope that she soon completes her research and logs the cache. You know it is a good cache when you want share it with other cachers and experience it some more.

Just got the okay to log. This was a distinctive, instructive, and very pleasurable multi, both novel and poetic, which I combined with three others. Parking a problem? Just think of what you'd be up against with a horse-drawn carriage. There are lots of geocaches that, after you're finished, you're glad you attempted, but there aren't many about which you can say "I'm really glad I didn't miss that one." This is one of those. TFTC (thanks for the cache).

Just got the OK to log this one. I thought this one was going to be a good one when it started in a cemetery and I was right. I have to be honest the cache is a tough find but so rewarding when you find it. Thanks for the wonderful multi Angevine.

This was a fun one—we admit that we did not have to go to the cemetery as we could tell from the description where we needed to be. Finding the cache was another story. Or epic poem, perhaps? C kept the kids while D ran around looking about. Lots of muggles made this more difficult—perhaps noon on a Saturday is the wrong time to look for this one? Thanks for the find and the poetry lesson!

Come Fly With Me

I've always loved hawks.

I cannot remember when I first started noticing them, so the activity must be one of those shrouded in the mists of my childhood. But I cannot remember a time when my eyes did not automatically scan the skies while walking, in a car, on a bicycle. *Look up. You never know what you might see.*

They glide, most of the time, hawks do; majestic, circling on air

Come fly with me.

currents, looking below for their next meal. Once, on a trip to California, I sat behind a pilot in a glider, and as we circled lazily on one of those air currents, I looked below us and saw a hawk, doing exactly the same thing, sharing the upwind, sharing the lift.

Look up. Once you start noticing hawks, it's difficult not to keep seeing them.

All four of us—me, Paul, my stepson Jacob, my stepdaughter Anastasia—were walking through the woods at Pawtuckaway State Park when something screamed, loud and high-pitched and wild, from somewhere off to our right. A chipmunk shot across the path in front of us and streaked up a tree, still screaming all the way. A heartbeat behind it was the hawk, silent, fast, flying down among the trees, a mere few feet above our heads.

The chipmunk lived; the hawk went hungry. It spread its wings and floated up to a thick solid tree branch just down the trail where it perched, still looking around for prey, its gaze steely. It ignored us as Anastasia and I approached, slowly and carefully, and stood directly below it. *Look up.*

Anything can happen when you're out geocaching. Anything.

Anything can happen; but you'll find that the most wonderful things happen when you go with an open mind and light tread. You have to remember that this isn't your world. When you go into the woods, you're interrupting a vast intricate web of life that goes on out there, every day and every night, through heat waves and snow and wind and rain and the few—the very few—really, really fine times. We walk into the woods as though we own them, seeking that one box of trinkets, that one human artifact that someone has placed there for us to find, our heads bent over our GPS receivers, our thoughts intent on its signals. We'd do better to go there gently, reverentially, trying to interrupt the flow of that life going on around us as little as possible, and grateful to have the opportunity to walk in the middle of it all. My friend Neil Rosen told me once, "you really notice things." I'd like to think that we all can: that we can all go into the woods or walk by the sea or sit by a lake and notice it all: the sounds and the smells, the feelings, the whispers that have nothing to do with human voices.

Mary Votava used the old cliché of stopping to smell the roses; but what we need to remember is that clichés become so ragged and tattered for the very good reason that they speak truths. Geocaching gives you the opportunity—the excuse, perhaps, if you need one—to slow down. To be aware of your surroundings, the air, the light, the sounds, the taste. To be aware of *yourself* in those specific surroundings: your breathing, how you feel, what the particular space you're in awakens within you.

Now—*look up.*

A Conversation with Dave Ulmer

Dave Ulmer, as we have seen, is the individual who first "invented" the hobby of geocaching. It was not his first invention, and while it was not he who followed through with it and brought it to the success it enjoys today, his contribution is nonetheless very important.

Why do you geocache?
I geocache to find unusual historical or geographic locations.

What is your style of caching . . . how do you "play the game?"
I rarely "play the game"—rarely even find the cache. Just explore the area.

What is the most moving or magical thing that has happened to you when geocaching? Can you share that experience?
Having the first stranger, Mike Teague, find my first cache. That was a thrill.

Do you experience geocaching as being part of a community? If so, in what way(s)? Have people from the community become your friends?
No, I'm pretty much a loner and am working on a more important invention.

What sorts of things do you pick up? What do you leave behind?

TNLN (take nothing, leave nothing)

How do you feel when you geocache?

Curious.

You began the whole hobby of geocaching. What led you to think of it? Can you tell readers a little of the story that brought the hobby into being?

The Navy removed the jamming signal from the GPS satellite system and increased the accuracy tenfold. That event I watched happen right on the screen of my GPS. That night I thought that there must be some "totally new" thing that humans can do now that they can find a spot to within thirty feet. I brainstormed all the possibilities and a Treasure Hunt came to mind. The next day I put out the first cache.

You later had concerns about the potential damage that the hobby can cause the environment. What were those concerns? Have they come to pass?

Damage has been minor. Geocaching.com has done a good job at policing caches and protecting the environment.

You left the hobby for a number of years, and now are back. Why did you leave, and why did you return?

Never totally left, never totally returned. I'm busy on a book I'm writing. I live full-time in a motor home towing a trailer with dirt bike and snowmobile. These toys keep me really busy exploring the remote areas of the Western U.S. The nearest geocache is some 16 miles and it's just a dumb roadside box. I don't feel like putting geocaches at my favorite spots like the hot spring I am at now. I do interviews about geocaching almost weekly. Just finished one talking from a nearby mountaintop to the Canuks at the CBC over my cell phone.

In many ways it seems that you should be the person currently "running" geocaching. Were you not interested in it? Or do you feel that it was taken away from you?

Geocaching is a minor invention for me. ISSU has been my big project for some 20 years and will continue to be the most important thing in my life for many years to come.

(Not long after this interview, I wrote a short article for a blog in a different context in which I talked about a good idea not being enough— that the idea has to be developed, followed through, etc. Although Dave Ulmer didn't develop the geocaching concept, we all owe him a great deal for having originated it.)

FOUR

Geo-Events

History, we can confidently assert, is useful in the sense that
art and music, poetry and flowers, religion and philosophy
are useful. Without it—as with these—life would be poorer
and meaner; without it we should be denied some of those
intellectual and moral experiences which give meaning
and richness to life. Surely it is no accident that the
study of history has been the solace of many
of the noblest minds of every generation.

—HENRY STEELE COMMAGER (1902–1998)

Bread and Roses

Three times a year on a Wednesday night, the back room of the
Shaskeen, an Irish pub on Elm Street in Manchester, New Hampshire, comes alive with talk of . . . geocaching.

Geocoins are brought, displayed, exchanged. A table is filled
with travel bugs (especially ones that are specifically created to
move from event to event) waiting to get picked up and moved
along. Stories and directions are swapped. Prizes are given out;
directions to night caches distributed. Guinness beef stew, fish and

chips, and bangers and mash are eaten. A very fair amount of beer is consumed.

Welcome to *Bread and Roses,* a geo-event that Paul and I started and that may well continue once we're long gone, as it appears to have taken on a life of its own.

As you've probably gathered by now, the notion of place is extraordinarily important to me. There's an ethos of place as well as of time, a way that our surroundings become a part of us and influence who we are and what we do. I explore this a lot in the fiction that I write, and everything I do is in some way affected by where I am. It's one reason that I spend two months out of the year in Provincetown, on the very tip of Cape Cod, a place that lifts my spirits, rekindles my passions, nurtures my soul, and inspires my writing.

When Paul and I moved to Manchester, we were both profoundly affected by the space in which we found ourselves. Paul responded by becoming an expert on the surrounding wooded area (so much so that one geocacher has facetiously rechristened nearby Lake Massabesic as "NotTheLake" in honor of Paul's NotTheP-ainter geo-name). I responded by turning to one of my passions, history, and delving into the city's past. The tribal or First Nations names that surrounded us captivated me: Piscataquog, Pawtuck-away, Ashuelot, Contoocook, Pigwacket, Pisgah.

But mostly it was with a mixture of horror and fascination that I approached a far more recent history.

Situated on the Merrimack River with shallow, fast-moving water and only sixty miles from Boston, Manchester developed rapidly, especially after the Civil War, and quickly established itself as the country's textile capital, surpassing its twin city in England for which it had been named. In 1838 the Amoskeag Manufacturing Company was established; it didn't close its doors until 1936.

The Amoskeag had a network of thirty mills, geographically

close to each other, that produced cotton and woolen textile products. Around the turn of the century, the company was the largest textile producer in the world, employing some 17,000 workers in its mills in Manchester and covering 1,500 miles of floor space; five million yards of cloth were exported every week. Every *week*.

So much for the statistics.

I walked down to the river—mills always used the power of the rivers to run—and stood looking up at the uniform gargantuan red brick buildings. Rows and rows of floor-to-ceiling windows stared impassively back.

They didn't open those windows, did you know that? They didn't open the windows, no matter how hot the summer—and inland New England gets very hot and humid in the summer—because of contaminants that could hurt the textiles. Add to that the layers of clothing that people, particularly women, had to wear, the long work hours spent standing and working heavy machinery in rooms where the noise level was, quite literally, deafening, and you begin to have a sense of what it was like to live in Manchester a century ago.

Yet they flocked to the mills. In various "old countries" the call was heard: the streets, they were told, were paved with gold; and perhaps when compared to what poverty and devastation the new immigrants left behind, they were. Especially in Manchester, where labor organization and strikes were averted by the mill companies' generous benefits, which were in fact far better than most of us receive from our employers today.

Women in particular found working the mills liberating. I pictured them, too, their long hair tied back in kerchiefs, women who for generations had been dependent on fathers and husbands, slaves in their homes, at the economic mercy of men for whom they were no more than any other possession.

Now suddenly they could see the value and worth of their labor;

they brought home their own money; they formed friendships with other women that would have been impossible in their worlds before that.

But the hours were long, twelve and fourteen-hour days, and the workers died young. The river flooded and flooded again. Hard economic times came, and workers' pay was cut even as their workloads increased. The unions finally came to Manchester, but they came too late. The mills all moved south . . . and on Christmas Eve of 1939 the Amoskeag closed its doors forever.

I stood there in front of the mill and saw these people, coming out from the red brick buildings at the end of the day, grimy and exhausted. I stood there as they filed by me, the children still somehow finding the energy to run and shout, the men carrying their lunch pails, the women with a hand in the small of their backs, perhaps, going home to cook dinners and wash dishes and mend clothes.

I watched them go by, and I knew I couldn't not write about them.

In the meantime, Paul and I had attended our first geocachers' get-together, an orchestrated affair ably hosted by BigRock95, and thought it might be fun to try our hand at hosting one as well. In another odd moment of synchronicity, a new Irish pub had recently opened in Manchester, owned by the same people who own our favorite pub in Cambridge, making our new home feel a little more like our old one. We quickly and easily reserved the back room, and decided—in view of my recent interest in the city's past—to give our event a Manchester theme. We called it *Bread & Roses* as a nod to all the other mill towns that had in fact had to go on strike; see Appendix D for the announcement, which we placed online— events are listed as caches, which are then archived after the event has taken place.

Geo-events can be whatever you want them to be. What we wanted was an event that had some shape, some purpose, some meaning, as well as being a time for hanging out with others from the geocaching community.

Since prizes are popular with any group, we started by soliciting (and in some cases securing) donations: from Groundspeak itself, from GPS manufacturers, and from outdoor clothing, camping, and other such companies. In many cases this is a frustrating endeavor: donations are often earmarked over a year in advance, yet Groundspeak doesn't allow caches to be announced that far in advance, and the donating companies often require proof that such an event actually will be taking place. . . and on and on, in a circular Catch-22 kind of experience.

However, Groundspeak was generous, in particular giving us a stuffed Signal frog we've kept and used on our sign-in table at all subsequent events. Garmin responded, as did Backcountry.com—which was particularly generous and supportive—and since then we continue to add sponsors to the list. At some events we draw names for the prizes, at others we give them based on special events or qualities (for someone who has created a particularly special cache, for a woman whose husband had recently died, for someone who had just found their first cache, etc.).

I also stick to our theme and give a very short talk—"Jeannette's Patented Two Minutes of History"—that some people appreciate and that others simply endure. We make announcements as needed, and then hand out special caches that were created for *Bread & Roses* and that just went "live" that evening. Some people scramble to be first-to-find for these caches; others stay for another beer or two. One of the events is held in February—and New Hampshire in February can be bitterly cold—and still around eighty people regularly show up for it.

If you plan to hold an evening event such as this one, a little planning will make your life easier. Arrange with the pub/restaurant ahead of time that no tabs should be run, but that people should pay when they are served. This keeps confusion (and forgetting to pay one's bill) to a minimum. Tip the servers well, especially if you plan to return to the venue. Make sure you have nametags—yeah, they're a little dorky, but these are people you only know through reading logs: most people don't post their pictures on the geocaching site. By the same token, instruct people to use their geocaching name on their nametags, or both: most people sign logs only with their geocaching name, so calling them "John" or "Susie" is not particularly helpful.

Make sure you have a logbook and plenty of pens. Set aside space for coats in the wintertime, and have a designated space for travel bugs (these are objects that travel from cache to cache; see glossary for more details) to live as they pass through. Have both a beginning and ending time—in my experience, people will ignore both of them, but at least that gives *you* some parameters.

If you want to give out prizes, request donations as far ahead of time as possible, and don't neglect local shops, restaurants, and services. There can be all sorts of tie-ins to geocaching if you're creative enough about it, and it's *always* a good idea to drive income to local businesses.

Most of all, though, have fun!

CITO Events

One of the adages of geocaching is "cache in, trash out."

There are obvious environmental concerns about unleashing a lot of people into the woods, though in general geocachers have shown themselves to be careful and courteous visitors. Caches are prohibited from being placed in fragile environments, and when a cacher finds one that has been inexplicably approved in a place where the environment could be adversely affected, he generally tells the cache-hider, who (again, usually) removes the cache.

What people forget is that there are natural geo-trails through the woods, paths used by animals (as one sees from the presence of scat), and that passage along these trails is not harmful. Moreover, while some have expressed concerns about bushwhacking, the reality is that we're not talking about hundreds of people trampling through the forests here. A little bushwhacking is not harmful and can in fact, it appears, be helpful.

Paul had been asked by the New England Forestry Foundation to place a cache in one of their forests to help raise public awareness of the area's availability to those wishing to explore nature; the foundation exists to conserve New England forests. We had the opportunity as part of this project to meet Si Balch, the Director of Forest Stewardship, who took us on an extended nature walk, identifying trees, birds, and wildlife alike as we went.

What amazed me was how he walked through the area: Paul and I were gingerly picking our way around branches and bushes, stepping carefully over felled trees; he walked as though down a city street, crushing whatever happened to be under his feet. It was all part of the process of growth and regeneration of the forest, he explained; and I haven't minded bushwhacking so much after that.

The transitory nature of forests, particularly here in the U.S. Northeast, has never stopped amazing me. If you're at all familiar with New England, you have no doubt often seen old stone walls running beside roads, then veering suddenly off into the woods. If you were to follow them, you'd find them marking out spaces, sometimes with stones dislodged by roots or trees, falling apart in places, but *there*. For me, the astonishment is always in realizing that two hundred years ago, there were no woods here. These were fields under cultivation, pastures where cows and sheep and horses grazed, land open to the sky.

(I have the same feeling, though perhaps in reverse, when I find myself in the windblown supposedly changeless dunes of the Cape and realize that this area was once heavily forested, until the first settlers from England felled all the trees to send back to the companies that had paid for their passage.)

The lesson here, of course, is that nothing is as venerable as we think. The only constant in life is change; and yet it is what we resist the most, which shows how stubborn and ultimately not very bright our species tends to be. Here people once worked the soil, and it has now become a tangle of thicket and fallen leaves, haphazard branches and towering white and red pines, the squirrels and the woodchucks and the deer making it their home, where once domesticated animals were penned.

The homes that we spend so much money purchasing and furnishing and decorating and maintaining and showing off—where will they be two hundred years from now? The things we think we want to buy, the mergers we want to facilitate, the power we seek to obtain and maintain—in two hundred years, none of it will mean a thing. What an odd way to invest our time, when you really think about it.

There's nothing like sitting on a ruined wall in the middle of a forest to gain some perspective on change.

It was in this same forest that I came upon the ruins of an entire farm complex. The above-ground walls and roofs had long since disappeared, but the foundations were all there, and the doorways, and a well. It was a known archaeological site; the family's name was recorded. I sat there among the ruins and imagined them, too, coming and going in these woods that were not then woods. Here and there an artifact remained: pieces of iron in curious shapes, shards of old pots. The everyday implements of life.

In a digression from a digression, I will tell you about my greataunt, happy and secure for sixty years in a lesbian partnership which most of my family steadfastly and stonily ignored for much of my life. Her partner was an artist, and in the 1920s they traveled together, extensively, so that Aunt Edna could find the elements of nature that she transferred so seamlessly onto paper: flowers, moths, trees, shells. There were lots of stories, too, my favorite being of them skinny-dipping off the side of a cacique in the Aegean Sea . . . they brought back gifts from these travels, too, for this was a time before it was illegal to take artifacts from their countries of origin. From them I received a small clay oil-lamp, first century, the kind of oil-lamp that would have been present by the dozens in every household . . .

I hold that lamp, sometimes, nestling it in the palm of my hand; and I wonder about the woman or women who lit it at twilight in some distant hot land. Josephine Tey once wrote that history is not in accounts but in account-books, and she was right: this is real history, not history as we read it, history that's been written by the winners—this is something else, the real history of how people lived and what was important to them.

I sat on the cellar steps of that farmhouse and imagined them. If I closed my eyes, I could almost hear their voices . . .

While we were in the forest, we came upon a place frequented by the town's current youth, complete with an old mattress (and frame, brought in by some enterprising and hoping-to-get-lucky young man, no doubt) and strewn about with beer cans.

Paul, feeling some pride of ownership for having the first cache in this particular forest, immediately decried the mess. And so he organized his first CITO event: people getting together to clean up a geocaching area. In this case, someone with a *truck* getting together with them to clean up the area!

CITO events can be simple—you come, you clean, you leave. Some people like to make a party of them, complete with picnic or cookout where appropriate, sometimes with geocaches going live at the same time so that there can be a hunt—the limits are, once again, only the limits of your imagination.

Every year there's an International CITO Day, which may be well worth your involvement (you can find out the date at geocaching. com). There is something unique, I think, about doing something positive and feeling a connection with people all over the world who are doing the same positive thing at the very same time: a sense that we are all, truly, in this together.

And if people all over the planet can cooperate in something like cleaning up trash, imagine what more we could do! There's a vision here of something that could grow, something that could generate more cooperation, more community work . . . something that could, maybe, change the world.

I believe that everyone who geocaches, no matter where, is constantly and soberly aware of the amount of trash with which people pollute the world. I've seen people take fast-food containers from the floors of their cars and transfer them to the ground outside and drive off without a second thought. It is completely amazing to me how some individuals can have such a narrow sense of their surroundings that all that matters to them is their possessions—not even the immediate area they frequent.

Perhaps pollution, like beauty, is in the eye of the beholder; but what I will promise you is that once you've started geocaching, you will develop keen eyes and a deep need to get rid of all the soda cans, candy wrappers, and so on that you see around you.

I'd also like to introduce another concept that I've been thinking about lately—that perhaps there is a parallel somewhere between physical waste and mental/spiritual waste. That perhaps cleaning up our world is not a bad start for cleaning our minds, cleaning our souls. We carry so much garbage around inside ourselves—negative feelings, resentment, anger, pain, guilt. It's garbage that we hold on to because we don't know how to get rid of it. We turn to religions, therapists, sports, love affairs, careers . . . anything that will take our minds off the garbage inside us.

But garbage pollutes. It pollutes the earth and it pollutes the body and it pollutes the soul. And the only way to get rid of it is to get rid of it. Let your time in the woods be a time where you can consider your own garbage, the garbage you carry around with you, and the garbage that you hand to other people—as we all do at one time or another. Use your time to decide what you want to do about it, and make a plan to do it.

In Nepal they speak of spiritual pollution; there is even an obscure goddess who is charged with helping people with their spiritual pollutants. We may not all have a Chwwaassaa Dyo with us, but we can use the woods, the solitude or the companionship we find there, to really examine all our rubbish.

Put some trash bags in your backpack, and don't be too discouraged if they fill up quickly and need to be replaced often. Remember that you're leaving the area a better place than you found it.

Part of opening your heart to nature is taking care of it, too.

Other Geo-Events

There are events being dreamed up as I write this, I'm quite sure of it, so by the time you read it, I'm pretty sure that someone will be doing something creative somewhere near you. I was reading the geocaching.com forums today and saw a proposal being floated for a global geo-event, which could be really interesting, though the logistics of it cause the mind to boggle.

There are mega-events, with more than five hundred people attending; the famous GeoWoodstock is one such event. There are group outings organized to tackle particular caches. In Germany, a group has organized to go "caching under the stars"—night geo-caching can be a lonely and frightening event (I once did it right beside a cemetery, which will really test your nerves) so maybe doing it *en masse* isn't a bad idea!

People combine geocaching with other events: church youth groups and Boy and Girl Scouts organize outings as part of their programs, and groups in Yosemite and Maine are combining geocaching with a road rally, a particularly creative and appropriate idea.

There is a substantial section on the geocaching.com site dealing with group and organized geocaching endeavors, so if that's your area of interest, read about it, and join the discussion in the appropriate forums.

It is our task-our essential, central, crucial task-to transform ourselves from mere social creatures into community creatures. (M. Scott Peck)

Remember that events are first and last about community. Being brought together by a common interest is as good a reason for forming a community as any other, and bonding through common experiences will make that community stronger. Yes, it has all the drawbacks of a community, too—we've never yet put on an event without somebody complaining about *something*—but that's part of human nature, and fighting it is like fighting the tides. Water will always win. Instead, smile and shrug and spare some sympathy for someone who needs to be negative to feel alive.

And if you do feel bad, I have a great cure: go out and look for a cache!

INTERLUDE

A Conversation with Jerry Carter

Jerry lives in Stokesdale, North Carolina, where he works in transportation management.

"I discovered geocaching in June of 2001 accidentally while chasing links on the Internet," Jerry explains. "My wife loves to hike, I need a reason, and we both love gadgets. It was a match made in heaven. We found our first cache on Kathie's birthday June 30, 2001.

"I have a physical condition that limits my caching, but not my love for the sport/game/hobby," says Jerry. He responded by starting to create hiking sticks, each adorned with the Groundspeak logo, and "I started the first online magazine dedicated to geocaching (todayscacher.com) in January 2004, even though I knew nothing about creating magazines, writing, publishing etc. I do know how to put a team of people together that do know these things. The magazine is made up of volunteer cachers that share the same love of geocaching as I do.

So . . . how are you involved in geocaching?

In June of 2002 I ordered a custom-made hiking staff over the Internet and when I received it I thought that I could do that better. A month later I hid a cache to celebrate the hundredth find of two cachers that I knew. I wanted to give them a nice prize for reaching this important milestone. After some thought I decided to make them each a hiking staff to commemorate the event. They were so well received that I sent a picture of them to Geocaching.com asking permission to use the Geocaching logo on hiking staffs. They loved the idea and a partnership was born!

At first the orders were slow but as time went by more and more people saw them at events and began to order. The original staffs are crude compared to what I create now. As with anything the more you do it, the better you get at it. I started off just making staffs with the Geocaching logo and the name of the cacher, and of course my trademark the pitchfork. Then I had a lady ask if I could put a Tufted Titmouse on the staff. I tried it and it came out fairly good.

When I posted the picture of the staff on my website [geo-hiking-stick.com] the floodgates opened. It wasn't long that I became overwhelmed with people wanting one of my staffs. The artwork was and still is my biggest challenge. I've never considered myself an artist so I'm always very apprehensive and overly critical of my work. To this day I'm still nervous when I open an email from a buyer after they have received their staff. I'm always afraid that it didn't meet their expectations.

So far I've had nothing but positive responses. Except for the time I misspelled the cacher's name, and unfortunately it was a Christmas present from her brother. She now has two staffs!

When I decide to create a staff I don't just pick up a piece of wood and start. I will sometimes spend hours looking at a raw staff, imagining in my mind what it will look like when completed, and then try to pick the one I think best fits the buyer. I will walk with it to see how it feels in my hands, and when I'm comfortable with it and know all of its curves and knots I will start to work. I have raw staffs that have been in my shop for years that I still haven't found a fit for. There's nothing wrong with them, it's just that the person they belong to hasn't come along yet. It typically takes from six to ten hours to complete a staff from beginning to end. The hardest part is shipping them off. Even though it has someone else's name on it, I still feel like it's mine.

I've always given away or donated many more staffs than I've sold. I'd rather make one for a friend or to donate one to an event or for a charitable reason, rather than sell one. I've made two staffs for *Make a Wish Foundation* that raised over two thousand dollars. The personal gratification that I derive from this far surpasses any I get from selling them. However, the cost of giving them away is sometimes more than I can afford, so on occasion I will sell one. I keep trying to retire from making staffs, but people won't let me.

I went to Geo Woodstock III in May of 2005, and I was amazed at the number of people walking around with one of my staffs. It gave me a huge sense of pride! Due to the demand and time restraints, I pick and choose who I will make a staff for. I would love to make one for everyone that requests one, but it's just not possible. I have to be in the mood to create a staff. I can't just print off an order and go to work. If I don't enjoy working on them, I don't work on them. Therefore the turn-around time on my staffs is from ninety days to six months.

FIVE

Inconveniences

It has been said that trees are imperfect men, and seem to
bemoan their imprisonment rooted in the ground. But they
never seem so to me. I never saw a discontented tree. They
grip the ground as though they liked it, and though fast rooted
they travel about as far as we do. They go wandering forth in
all directions with every wind, going and coming like
ourselves, traveling with us around the sun two million miles a
day, and through space heaven knows how fast and far!
—JOHN MUIR (1838–1914)

In every activity, there have to be some limits. Some policing.
Some Bad Things.

So I'm starting this chapter with a look at the guidelines and
restrictions placed on geocaching—things that geocachers like to
talk about *ad infinitum, ad nauseaum*—and from there will move into
injuries and other things that geocachers *don't* like to talk about.

You've had the falling dream, right? The one where you're going
off a cliff, or down a hole, or something like that? I've been having
those dreams for years, and I will admit—I've been places geocaching that fit quite nicely into that particular nightmare. So it's

another word to the wise: exercise caution out there. Don't go too close to the edge, wherever you are.

That's not bad advice for life, actually. Enjoy the view . . . but don't go too close to the edge.

And for those who do want to get too close to the edge—well, I've included a note about extreme caching here, too. So if you want to go the psycho route, geocaching has something for you.

Don't look at me: I'm not getting even *near* that edge!

Guidelines

There is endless discussion of geocaching guidelines on the forums, and it's a fair bet that any guideline, at one time or another, has been under attack by someone. Moreover, they do change from time to time, usually in response to a problem. In the resources section in the back you'll find a website that posts the newest geocaching guidelines; it's well worth checking out.

The first and most obvious guideline to follow involves local laws and ordinances. Geocaching is done all over the world, and everywhere it's done a little differently.

In the United States, geocachers are prohibited from placing caches in National Parks and indeed on any federally owned land. This is unfortunate in view of the vast expanses of national parks that would provide very fertile ground indeed for such an enterprise.

The geocaching.com site maintains cache listing requirements and guidelines at geocaching.com/about/guidelines.aspx.

The list of current prohibitions includes caches on land maintained by U.S. Park Service; buried caches; caches that deface property; caches on archaeological or historical sites; caches hidden in close proximity to active railroad tracks (if you can't figure out why, you probably shouldn't be geocaching at all—though, strangely, the commonsense reason is not the real reason for railroad tracks being banned. They are often on private ground with a right of way for the tracks that does not extend to pedestrians on or near the tracks!); caches on or near military installations; and caches near or under public structures (highways, dams, bridges, government buildings, schools, airports) that could be targets for terrorist attacks.

The site page also reminds cachers of some commonsense considerations that are often forgotten—that non-geocachers could easily find some of our behavior peculiar or even dangerous, and that minimizing this perception is in everyone's best interests.

Reviewers

There are a number of cache reviewers who judge whether or not a cache meets the current Groundspeak guidelines. Their word, essentially, is the last word on the subject. Don't want to play by our rules? Fine: go play someplace else.

(People can and do appeal the reviewers' decisions, but the appeals are usually by new geocachers who have not read the guidelines, and the decisions are rarely overturned.) By and large, the approvers are human, geocachers themselves, and are applying the guidelines for the good of the geocaching community.

How do you get to be an approver? Not by competing for the position. In one of Robert Heinlein's books, the desire to become president automatically disqualified the person from the job (not a bad idea at all, in my humble opinion: I'd love to see it imposed posthaste in the United States—the whole fabric of politics would change!). Groundspeak took a page from that book and chooses its approvers/reviewers following requirements that are not divulged to geocachers and have nothing to do with the desire for the volunteer position.

As you can imagine, people are constantly snarling at reviewers, as people tend to snarl at anybody in any position of authority. One must have, it seems to me, either an infinite supply of patience or a very thick hide. My conversation with Brad Webb (gpsfun) illuminates one reviewer's response to the controversies constantly swirling around him.

One of the problems is that reviwers are allowed some latitude in their decisions and "rulings," which of course means making a judgment call. It's a problem because judgments are always open to debate. At some point they must, of course, pull out the "because I said so" that is every parent's last resort; the comparison is surprisingly apt. If you don't believe me, spend some time on the forums. People can be infinitely silly, and egos are sometimes easily bruised.

With that flexibility in mind, we can see that in general, here's what reviewers do:

- plot cache locations and check for stupidity in cache placement (mistakes can place a cache in the middle of a four-lane highway)

- check for stupidity and plot caches

- make sure cache adheres to guidelines

- check that the area is not already saturated with caches

- look for caches needing maintenance

- make sure a proposed cache is not within 500 feet of another cache (it should be noted that this is one place where gpsfun cut me a little slack—one of the waypoints on my *Dark Satanic Mills* cache is also—and was first—one of the waypoints of another multi-cache called *Bronze and Stone*. It is the statue of a mill girl, critical to both our multis, and gpsfun kindly allowed it.)

- archive caches as needed

- hold or share no opinions as to the quality of any cache (Ground-speak has long resisted an oft-proposed plan for ranking).

Extreme caching

There's a subset of geocaching that is designed for the truly brave, the truly daring, and the truly insane, known unofficially as extreme caching.

Why did I place it in the chapter dealing with inconveniences? I have nothing against extreme caching; frankly, I stand in awe of anyone attempting it. But whereas I can take off for a couple of hours and slip into the woods and find a cache, extreme cachers need days, weeks, even months to plan a campaign. They need to take time out of their lives to execute the caches; often they have to travel some distance to get to the cache, and spend a not insignificant amount of money on equipment and vehicles to retrieve it.

I'd consider that inconvenient.

Extreme caching generally involves placing caches in seriously difficult-to-reach places that involve extreme procedures for retrieval that may involve the use of wetsuits, mountain-climbing gear, and helicopters. The Vinny-and-Sue Team is famous for placing a series of "Psycho Urban Caches" that are well worth reading about, if not actually pursuing. Read more about them in the conversations shared elsewhere in this book.

Note that this is not subtitled "stupid caching." That's something else altogether, wherein people place caches in seriously difficult-to-reach places that involve the attention (in the United States, anyway) of police, Homeland Security officials, and/or bomb squads. Let's be serious: you're putting an ammunition box under the supports for a bridge that spans five hundred feet over a river, carrying three lanes of traffic each way, twenty-four hours a day, *and you think that this is a good idea*?

The geocaching site tells you not to do that. Your common sense tells you not to do that. Law enforcement people tell you not to do that.

Don't do that.

Night Caching

This falls under the category of sometimes-inconvenient potentially dangerous caching. But there's a whole world out there just waiting for the night owl (I confess to being one) to explore.

I have to admit: I'm actually pretty terrified about going out into

Night caching

the woods at night. Not for any of the sensible reasons: I don't think about what might happen, like a twisted ankle or running into something bigger than myself or even getting lost. No: my fears don't come from the woods themselves, but from the many authors who have addressed what is actually in the other forest—the one we all keep inside our minds. One of my favorite authors is Phil Rickman, who explores the supernatural in ways to make it seem quite natural and extraordinarily appalling; his words are always with me once it's quite night outside.

A poet I can no longer identify wrote that we fear all the wrong things: we're afraid of ghosts when it's "men in steel, with iron purposes" who we should really fear. He is correct. But that doesn't banish the ghosts from our minds and going out into the dark encourages that useless fanciful thinking.

Not that the woods themselves don't provide enough of a backdrop for scary thoughts. Noises that no one would think to notice during the day are amplified as emotions are attached to them; the night-folk, as John Masefield (there's one poet whose name I *do* remember) calls them, are alive and well and living their nocturnal lives all around the human who happens into their space. Not knowing is, at a very primal level, fearing.

So I won't say I'm not scared when I go night caching. But it's a *frisson* that isn't altogether unpleasant, not unlike reading a scary novel or watching a frightening movie. I love Hitchcock, for example: he really knew how to scare you, often by suggesting more than showing. And the woods at night are very, *very* good at suggesting . . .

Night caches are placed so that they can be found at night. It's really that simple. The cache hider knows that you cannot see beyond the range of your flashlight, so there are fewer "clever" hiding places with night caches. Generally your GPS receiver starts you off at a listed set of coordinates and you shine your flashlight into the woods. The light is caught by a reflector on a tree, and you set off toward that tree. Once there, you shine the light around you again until you see the next, and so on, working your way to the cache from reflector to reflector.

These specifically placed night caches are to be distinguished from night-caching in general, since almost any regular cache can be found at night as well, and many first-to-find hounds will venture out in the darkness when a cache has first been published.

Either way, it's not just reflectors that you see glowing in the dark. Interestingly—and counter-intuitively—one's vision is sharpened and heightened at night (though only in the lighted area, that is to say where the flashlight is shining). So you see much more than you might see during the day, but in a smaller, extremely focused area.

Shadows flee from you as you advance on the path, and there is always—always—the sense of being watched, probably because you are. For me this always takes the form of a creeping certainty that there is something behind me on the path, following me, and I often must stop and turn around and look, even though I *know* that nothing will be there. The feeling then abates for a few minutes before, invariably, returning again.

The maneuver, moreover, is usually not appreciated by my geocaching companions, who may find themselves walking forward into darkness while Jeannette checks the path behind!

If you're not afraid of the dark, it's a really interesting way to get in touch with the forest. If you're slightly afraid of the dark, it can be a titillating experience, dipping your toe as it were into the shallow end of Lake Fear. Don't read Phil Rickman (or, adds Jacob, Dean Koontz) before venturing out. And the same rules apply in duplicate here: go with someone, let someone know where you are, carry an extra flashlight, dress appropriately. This isn't the time to dash off *sans* supplies!

Injuries

So what is the potential for getting hurt?

Obviously if you've decided to do extreme caching, your tolerance for risk and possible injury is a lot higher than mine. But even on the most gentle of caches, injury can indeed be right around the corner. Sharing just a few of the "adverse events," as the medical establishment's newest euphemism would have it, I can tell you about all sorts of accidents: punctures (usually inflicted by branches), pulled muscles, broken bones, snakebite, sprains, and scrapes. Some have been spectacular: the geocacher in Washington state who broke three different bones in his arm; the fellow in Ontario who ripped his mouth (because of being clipped in to his bicycle pedals: something to think about!), the geocacher in South Dakota who fell down a hillside of slate tailings from a mine (have to find out more about *that* cache), somebody who managed to get stung in the *eyes* with nettles . . . and the list could go on and on.

And that's not to mention other risks. In the United Kingdom, a cache-hider was sued when someone claimed that he or she (the cache-hider never learned the plaintiff's identity) broke an ankle when trying to retrieve the cache. The suit was dropped, but—especially in the lawsuit-happy United States—one never knows when something like that might happen again.

Generally, however, one doesn't risk much more geocaching than one does with any moderately active sport or hobby. The issues are really grouped around *where* one is, and *with whom*, when/if one gets hurt. If you're well prepared and careful, there's no reason to let fear stand in your way.

I had a difficult time writing this chapter. I put it off until the very last minute—as I started it, my deadline for getting the book in the hands of the publisher was down to less than a week. I think that my problem wasn't that I didn't know what to say—it was, rather, that what I had to say had nothing to do with the essence of the book, its core, its central message, which is about opening your heart. This chapter was too practical. In ways, this chapter was too *secular.*

The point is, of course, that—as usual—the sublime and the mundane have to go hand in hand. Have you ever noticed how most spiritual traditions deal in many ways with the practical essence of life? Spells aren't about anything that isn't, at its essence, natural and ordinary. Christ performed his first miracle at a wedding. Most Hindu schools of thought teach that divinity is everywhere. All of these involve less-than-spiritual elements of life. Spittle and clay. Water and wine. Doesn't get much more basic than that.

Perhaps the message is that the practical *is* the spiritual.

And in the practical is the mystical. We've all, as Frederick Buechner has pointed out, experienced moments of wonder, moments of mysticism.

> Mysticism is where religions start. Moses with his flocks in Midian, Buddha under the Bo Tree, Jesus up to his knees in the waters of Jordan, each of them is responding to something of which words like shalom, oneness, God even, are only pallid souvenirs. Religion as ethics, institution, dogma, ritual, Scripture, social action, all of this comes later and in the long run maybe counts for less. Religions start, as Frost said poems do, with a lump in the throat—to put it mildly—with a bush going up in flames, a rain of flowers, a dove coming down out of the sky. "I have seen things," Aquinas told a friend, "that make my writings seem like straw."
>
> Most people have also seen such things. Through some moment of beauty or pain, some sudden turning of their lives, most of them have caught glimmers at least of what the saints are blinded by. Only then, unlike the saints, we tend to go on as though nothing has happened.

We are all more mystics than we choose to let on, even to our-selves. Life is complicated enough as it is.

But *where* do these moments happen? Generally in the midst of the bustle of everyday life with its practical obligations and mun-dane concerns. We discover wonder where we least expect it, and its impact on us is all the greater because of that.

Driving down to Connecticut very early one morning, I was privileged to see a mountain lion run across the highway well in front of me. I pulled over to the side of the road and tried to see where it was, but it had gone. The moment was just that—a moment—but it held the shimmering magic of a thousand such moments. People in New England simply don't see these animals often, or indeed ever, according to the wildlife folks who assure us that there are no wildcats in the Northeast.

But I know what I saw, and I will hold it forever in my heart.

And it happened when I least expected it, when I was sleepy and playing music and reaching for coffee, resenting being up so early, resenting the long drive to my client's office . . . and all of that *ennui* vanished in an instant when I saw the grace and beauty of that big cat. "All gone," as my mother used to say about scrapes she had bandaged. All gone.

In the shelter of each other, the people live. *(Gaelic proverb)*

For twelve years my closest companion was my cat, Spike. We were together before I met Paul, and neither of them was any too happy about including the other in his relationship with me. Each gave in, a little, with varying grace, once it was clear to each that I planned on being with both of them.

Spike gave me many wonderful gifts throughout our life together, and when he got sick with cancer and died, I was beyond grief. I was lying on my bed, sobbing, a few days after we buried him, when I felt him jump up at the foot of the bed as he had every evening before marching up to join me on my pillow. I looked, and, of course, there was no cat there.

But I know what I felt. I know it was real. I know it was Spike saying good-bye.

He didn't appear to me in a rainbow or in a church or in any of the other places where one might expect it. When I go to visit his grave and place yet another stone or shell on the cairn we've built there over time, I feel a sadness and a loneliness—but I don't feel *him.* It was in the ordinariness of my bedroom, in a utilitarian space we had shared, that I felt touched by his presence.

And that made it all the more real.

We are married to the earth and to the things of the earth, and the sooner we come to terms with that, the better off we all will be. We're approaching the point of no return in our relationship with our planet, and if we continue to pollute her atmosphere and waters, if we continue to drill into her and build cities on her and explode bombs in her islands and atolls, we won't ever be able to go back. Already we've lost much of our heritage: rain forests in the south given over to agriculture, pine forests in the north stripped for logging; oceans that have no fish left to give us; species that are becoming extinct at an alarming rate.

And yet this is precisely where we connect with ourselves, our hearts, and our communities. This is the crossroads of the spiritual and the secular, or the ordinary and the sublime: here, on earth. "I want to grow something wild and unruly," sings Natalie Maines, and that desire for wildness, for strangeness, is in all of us. Our attraction to the things of the earth isn't just about our physical survival; it's about our psychic survival as well.

This intersection takes place on nearly every level of our beings. People are often surprised to learn how intertwined are sexuality and spirituality; that it is the travelers of the interior who are often the most willing to break down sexual taboos as well. In *Exit to Eden*, Anne Rice blurs the act of taking sexual risks with taking philosophical ones, and they're not so far apart.

And, indeed, from time to time you'll see admissions on the geocaching forums that some couples' forays into the woods for a cache also often include a sexual encounter. It is natural to be moved by the stillness and the secretness and the life pulsing through the forest, the few wild places left in our lives. It makes far more sense to me to have passionate sex in the wilderness than in the prescribed suburban bedroom, the door primly closed, the blinds carefully drawn, the encounter timed and measured and stored up for later memories or arguments.

If that's the choice, I'll do it in the woods, thank you very much.

And as soon as I wrote that, I winced, the memory of too many times with too few precautions coming back to me. No, I'm not talking about safe sex in the usual sense; I'm talking about bug spray. Use the organic kind and use it liberally.

So as you see, we really do come full circle: I started talking about philosophy and ended up thinking about applying insect repellant to my backside. The sacred and the profane, all jumbled up together. Which is where they belong.

Any religion is incarnate in the earth. Every tradition has a creation myth, a reason why we're here. We usually like to think of the "we" in that equation: why *we*'re here. But shouldn't the question equally be posed, why we're *here*? What is it about our species and this planet that makes for such a love-hate relationship, that calls to us down the long flickering corridors of tribal memories, that binds us together even when we seek so desperately to escape the embrace?

What is it that makes us need the earth and yet yearn for the stars?

INTERLUDE

A Conversation with Paul Cézanne

Paul Cézanne is well known in the New England area and on the geocaching.com forums as NotThePainter; he is also the author's partner, and she thought it best, since readers have heard so much *about* him, that *he* get a chance to say how he feels.

Why do you geocache?

I started because it sounded like geeky fun. I thought I would like it because it would get me out into the woods, but I also like the "secret society" aspect of it. I also like that I get to spend time with my wife, and I get to spend time with my kids, doing something a little bit different.

I also get a big ego boost with my hides. I try to make hides that aren't lame, whether they are traditionals or my puzzles. I enjoy reading compliments in my logs.

What is your style of caching—how do you "play the game?"

I play many different games. Sometimes I just want to get out. I always enjoy a FTFP run. *(First to find published. See glossary for details.)* I'm often up at extremely early hours to grab the caches. (I don't enjoy solo night caching, otherwise I'd be out doing them, also!) I used to be into the numbers, but that stopped rather early on. Now I find it quite easy to drive by a simple cache and not worry about it. A cache either has to be worth going to, as defined by a good destination, hike, or in some cases puzzle, or it has to be part of a FTFP run, or even part of a numbers run. (I've gone on two of those: you set out early and try to collect as many caches as you can in a set period of time. They are a bit silly and I'm only interested in doing more if I can beat my previous twenty-four-hour record. A run that just gets more numbers without beating my personal best just isn't worth doing.)

Some caches I'll visit over and over again because I like the hike or the view. I rarely do those alone, I'll bring along a family member or a friend, and maybe even a bottle of wine to enjoy while watching the sunset.

What is the most moving or magical thing that has happened to you when geocaching? Can you share that experience?

I love driving toward the cache on a FTFP run and watching the sun rise around me. The word is so quiet and peaceful then.

Do you experience geocaching as being part of a community? If so, in what way(s)? Have people from the community become your friends?

Oh, yes, certainly. This was a big surprise to me. I don't make friends quickly or easily, and I'm really pretty content with just being with Jeannette most of the time. And yes, I have made many friends in the community; that has certainly made my life richer.

What sorts of things do you pick up? What do you leave behind?

I quickly became disillusioned about the crap that people leave. I don't trade except for coins and travel bugs. If a TB (travel bug) has a lame mission I'll just drop it in the next cache. If it has a good one, especially one that wants photographs, I'll keep it for a while, carrying it with me. *Plastic Jesus* was one of my favorites: you're supposed to take its picture in front of an artifact of any religion. I got a photograph of it near a statue of Ganesh!

How do you feel when you geocache?

Happy, unless I'm on a FTFP run, then I feel energized—I'm in a race. The adrenaline is high then. This actually causes mistakes. I'm known in the community for keying the number into my GPS receiver incorrectly in my haste, or not getting an important clue that was right on the cache page!

SIX

Don't Bug Me!

When I can go just where I want to go,
There is a copse of birch trees that I know;
And, as in Eden Adam walked with God,
When in that quiet aisle my feet have trod
I have found peace among the silver trees,
Known comfort in the cool kiss of the breeze
Heard music in its whisper, and have known
Most certainly that I was not alone!

—FATHER ANDREW (DATES UNKNOWN)

Travel bugs belong to the category of things known as hitch-hikers: objects that are on the move from cache to cache, following specific guidelines set up by the person sending the object out into the wild. They're another way of playing the game, of casting a little of oneself out into the world.

Travel bugs are identified by a special numbered dog tag purchased from Groundspeak. Anyone can buy a travel bug dog tag and attach it to any object, devising a mission for that travel bug as they wish. Paul has one attached to his stout walking stick; if a geocacher meets him out on the trail, he or she may log that travel bug.

An elementary school class sent out a travel bug with the instructions that it was to return to the classroom by the end of the school year; with the numbers inscribed on the dog tags, the class was able to monitor the travel bug's progress. Paul sent out a travel bug meant go to a cache in every city in the world called Manchester. Others, like the *Plastic Jesus* travel bug he cited in his interview, ask that photographs be taken of them and placed on the geocaching.com site.

Some want travel bugs to travel around the planet; some just want to travel from event to event. There are, in fact, special travel bugs that can only be exchanged at events, including one that is a floor lamp! There is a whole category of huge ones. Bowling balls are popular; telephones, cement blocks two yards tall, and an airplane propeller have all been made into bugs.

That's one of the things that people find fun—attaching the dog tag to clever and improbable objects. The pleasure can be in sending them out into the world . . . or in seeing exactly what people are willing to endure to log them. Some are silly (I scared my stepkids by placing a rather large snarling plastic rat in the linen closet. . . . it was a TB, temporarily in residence *chez moi* before moving on), some are eloquent, some are creative, some are innocuous.

Like the people who send them out.

People take the travel bug enterprise seriously, too. There's a travel bug graveyard, where folks can "bury" their travel bugs that have gone astray . . . and resuscitate them if for some reason the travel bugs return. Or they can be buried if they are, by their owner's determination, at the end of their lives. There are no limits to what a fanciful imagination can think of . . .

This is a place where owners of travel bugs that have "passed on" may bury and memorialize them. This gets deceased bugs off the cache pages as well as out of the owners' hands; while still main-

taining the history, logs, and finds for the bugs. Visitors and mourners alike may come here to visit and read the life stories of bugs that have been laid to rest.

In this cemetery, re-incarnation can happen. If you have buried a bug here but later decide to attach a copy of the tag to a new bug and release it, simply retrieve your bug from this cache and redeposit it wherever you have chosen for your bug to begin its new life.

When holding your funeral, please respect the sanctity of these hallowed grounds by logging your visit only as a note. "Found" entries upset the spirits and will be promptly deleted without notice.

To bury a dead bug here, make sure it is in your inventory and then post a note log here indicating what bug you are burying. When you post your note, select the bug you are burying from the "travelers" dropdown list and it will be deposited here when you post your log.

—Instructions from the Travel Bug Cemetery

Travel bugs are anther way of getting a bit of yourself out in the world and seeing where it will go. It's not an activity for control freaks, however, no matter how much they—we—really want to be in charge of the world.

Jeep Travel Bugs

Jeep travel bugs are a marketing scheme by Jeep—who else?—that have some geocachers delighted and others disdainful. They have their own special icons (white, yellow, and green, depending on the year), and some people like the "specialness" of these icons.

The first year they were yellow, the second year they were white, this year as I write this they are green. They are so coveted that some people don't pass them on, but rather hoard them, an unfortunate but possibly predictable byproduct of the presence of such a popular object.

Each year there is a contest where you take a photo of a Jeep Travel Bug and submit it to Jeep. There are all sorts of prizes . . . including, inevitably it seems, a real Jeep vehicle.

Jeannette and Travel Bugs

If you read about the cache I called *Like It Or Not,* you'll see it's a control freak's dream: do it my way, or I erase your log! There's part of me that still ardently believes that I could run the world quite fairly and efficiently, thank you, but fortunately there's another, healthier part of me that is gradually taking over: the part that realizes how little in life we do actually control and understands that the *desire* to control (like the desire for anything unattainable) works like poison in the system.

Desire itself is a double-edged sword; it feels okay, at first, but gradually desire becomes more important than all the other thoughts and feelings you might have, and it takes over. Eventually it can only be replaced with another desire, as attaining the thing or person or state that you wanted isn't as important as you thought it might be, and you set your sights on the next object of desire.

Not a healthy way to live.

Desire for control is one of the most insidious and seductive of all desires because many of us keep the illusion that we can actually attain it, despite all indications to the contrary. We live, for example, on a planet that is routinely devastated by nature—fires, floods, hurricanes, tornadoes. Many parts of the planet are uninhabitable because of extremes of terrain or temperature.

If that were not enough, we belong to a species that, symbolically at least, eats its young: people are marginalized, hurt, and even killed because of differences in skin color, sexual orientation, mental health, socioeconomic status, gender, and temperament. We tolerate levels of aggression and violence that would make Genghis

Khan blush, and in the same breath we assert that we are in control of our lives, our destinies, our professions, our children, our marriages, our love affairs . . . how wretchedly simplistic and blustery such a claim really is!

Yet I clung to it for a long time, and in some ways it is geocaching that really brought me face to face with the absurdity of the belief. The reality is that people simply will not behave the way I want them to in the geocaching community, and they really don't care what I think about them at all. Just as . . . wait for it . . . people will simply not behave the way I want them to in the human community, and *they* really don't care what I think about them at all, either.

Once when my stepdaughter Anastasia was five or six, she went into a tantrum when we wouldn't give her what she wanted. After pouting, tears, screaming, and the time-honored tradition of The Holding Of The Breath, she finally turned to Paul, stamped her foot, and exclaimed, "You're not making me happy!"

At some level we're all still there with Anastasia, aren't we? Still believing that the world should be fair and that all events should conspire to make us happy because, to borrow a line from the movie *Working Girl,* "I am, after all, me!"

That's where I've been, in any case, more often than I'd like to admit.

So I placed *Like It Or Not.* And then Paul gave me a set of travel bug tags for some occasion or the other, and I had to think of exactly what it was that I wanted to send out into the world, and with what mission. Travel bug tags are purchased from Groundspeak and are attached to the travel bug itself in some manner. They hold the identifying numbers (like military dog tags, which they resemble except for the spider logo they carry!) of the travel bug, enabling it to be logged, passed on, and its route followed.

I chose a small plastic toy—a sheep. I've always had a odd fondness for sheep, mainly from a city-dweller's limited and romanticized perspective: at times when I've been in situations I haven't liked, I've fantasized about chucking it all and heading off to the country and raising sheep, which would (no doubt, I've assured myself) be far less stressful than whatever it was I was doing that was at that moment driving me crazy. Never mind the stressful reality of life on a farm: the fantasy endures, and I still think of them as the most peaceful of creatures.

Having my theme in hand, so to speak, I remembered with delight some of the comments I'd received about *Like It Or Not* and decided straightaway that my travel bug, too, should have a poetic requirement. From there it was just a short jump over to William Blake and his *Little lamb, who made thee?*—and so my travel bug was born. Paul drilled a hole in the plastic sheep; I threaded the dog tag through and wrote up my instructions (see page 96).

It went "live" at a *Bread & Roses* event and was eagerly claimed by the geocacher who had pronounced himself so besotted with *Like It Or Not* that he and his daughter had telephone conversations about poetry. My travel bug requirement—to read and comment specifically on Blake—was received with delight. Unable to pronounce himself, though, he gave up after about six months.

I should have gotten a clue then. I really should have.

But I didn't. It subsequently passed into the hands of a couple of geocachers who valiantly tried to fulfill its mandate, into the hands of a couple of geocachers who ignored its mandate altogether (and whose TB logs I mercilessly excised from the geocaching.com site), and finally into the hands of some unknown geocacher who apparently got so fed up with the whole enterprise he or she took it out of circulation altogether.

I felt enraged. I felt deflated. I cried.

Paul, fresh from his morning meditation (how infuriating those who are calm and collected are to those of us who are not!), took a predictably Zen-like approach to my issue: "Expecting people to do what you want them to sets you up for disappointment," he said. "Just send things like that out and see what happens to them. That can be just as much fun."

Just as much fun as forcing people to read something they don't want to read? Could it be? The mind boggled.

Okay, so you're right: I'm making fun of myself here. My travel bug experience, however, fit in nicely with other events in my life at the time that all had to do with lessons the Universe was teaching me about letting go, and it seemed, somehow, meant.

Its not that I'm advocating giving up responsibility; if anything, there seems to me to be more emphasis on responsibility when you start accepting that the only control you have is over your own responses to the world. Oh, you can make plans; you can get married, write a book, start a company, adopt a child. But marriages end, books get rejected, companies fail, children disappoint. At the end of the day you had less control over all of those events than you ever thought you did.

But you do have to take responsibility for your thoughts, your actions, your lapses in judgment, your failures to communicate. You may well have contributed to the marriage ending, the book being rejected, and so on. You contributed; you weren't in control. That's the difference.

Send the little lamb out into the world and see where he goes, what adventures he has, what people he meets, what places he sees. Enjoy his travels, and all the things he touches.

And don't try and play king of the world. It never works.

Little lamb, who made thee?
Travel Bug

Current Goal: "Little lamb, who made thee?" is the beginning of a poem by William Blake. This little lamb likes poetry and can only travel if you're willing to read some!

Here's the Scoop: Send me an e-mail telling me which of Blake's poems you like the most and why. (If you log this travel bug without sending me the e-mail and having me approve your find, I'll remove your log, so let's not go there!) Once I've read your e-mail, you may take this little lamb wherever you'd like. He'll be happy to trot along!

Jana9

This Travelbug was released by an 8-year-old girl in April 2006.
It would like to visit Japan.

A Conversation with Vinny and Sue

The caching team of Vinny and Sue (they've chosen to keep their last names confidential in this book) is known throughout the geocaching world. They may have originated extreme caches; they certainly place them. These are caches that can be found only after a difficult climb, a helicopter ride, or other extreme forms of transportation. They are for a different group of geocachers altogether—the "extreme" teams.

Sue's Story

I bought Vinny a GPS receiver for his birthday in April 2005. I had not heard of geocaching, but Vinny had shown an interest in buying a GPSr (*shorthand for a GPS receiver*) when we were out shopping. I also thought the maps therein would help him when he drove to unfamiliar places (I didn't buy one with autorouting as they were out of my price range). I researched the different models unbeknownst to Vinny and not having much of a clue what he would use it for. I bought one on eBay, luckily choosing an excellent model for geocaching—Magellan Sportrak Pro.

Vinny was surprised . . . he played around with it, got a bit bored, started Googling and found geocaching.com. He had a vague memory of hearing about it before. He set up a geocaching.com account on April 24, 2005. On April 28, we went together and found out first two geocaches. Then we did the two closest to where we live in the Frederick Watershed. We went on from there, going out regularly to find one or two or three caches in Frederick to start with, learning geocaching tricks as we went. Vinny was more keen than I at first, then I discovered puzzle caches and generally became more interested. Vinny became more selective in the caches he wanted to find, more interested in extreme caches.

Why do you geocache?

. . . nice thing about this game, everyone wins . . . (someone may be faster than you, or find more than you, or you might DNF [*Did Not Find*], but you can almost always return to get a smilie)

. . . the challenge . . . of solving puzzles and finding devious hides, etc, saying "I did it," getting a brownie point.

. . . exercise and being in forests . . . only applies to some caches. I love being in forests, hiking through them, and caching makes it more interesting.

. . . sharing fun times and experiences with geocaching friends, making friends geocaching . . .

What is your style of caching . . . how do you "play the game?"

I go after the puzzle geocaches. I believe I have the top number of puzzle geocache finds out of Maryland cachers and Virginia cachers. I just recently passed GLM (a Virginia cacher) for number of puzzle cache finds, and he may get ahead of me again.

I cache regularly in Maryland, Virginia, and Pennsylvania. CCCooperagency of course is in Pennsylvania, so I have quite a way to go to beat her number of puzzle geocache finds!

What is the most moving or magical thing that has happened to you when geocaching? Can you share that experience?

This is a tough one to answer. Nothing really comes to mind as the most moving or magical . . .

. . . it may be watching Vinny as he creates Psycho Urban Caches and the attention and enjoyment people have got out of them. I have a little story about it on one of my cache pages (see "Sue's Puzzle Cache #3"). The first weekend the first of them was published, he met a bunch of cachers at one of them. He had a great time and was very happy and excited when he got home.

Then, later, we placed Psycho Urban Cache #8. Vinny had researched the site online before we went there in person. When we arrived, I was walking around saying "wow" over and over again at all the wonderful and interesting places to hide things! (It's at an old fort and there are many old concrete and wooden structures of varying shapes, sizes and purposes.) This cache was voted the best Maryland cache this year.

Then recently, on Psycho Urban Cache #13, Vinny didn't tell me what he had planned. He was inspired by caching friend LPYankeeFan's placement of the "Revenge of Team Psycho" cache just a week before. All of a sudden I hear him on the phone with a business that rents helicopters—surprise! He went out that afternoon, twice, in a helicopter, successfully placing the cache on top of an old railroad pylon in the middle of the Potomac River on the second trip. That was a big high for him in more ways than one!

The story of the only finders to date of this cache, "Team Psycho," is kinda moving, although I didn't have the opportunity to experience it in person (they didn't want anyone to know of their attempts until they had succeeded). They spend many hours over weeks planning how to retrieve the cache. They spent many hours on site over two prior weekends in unsuccessful attempts—and more hours in their successful attempt. They learned from their mistakes and had nightmares over it. They watched Vinny fly in by helicopter to do cache maintenance. There were nine team members. They had a leader, directing activity and assigning each member tasks. In the words of one of the team members, it was euphoric. While many cachers have spent many hours trying to solve tough puzzle geocaches (usually at home), I've not heard of any other joint efforts such as this—where such planning, preparation and teamwork was involved in the actual physical retrieval of the cache.

Anyway, aside from the Psycho Urban Caches, it's pretty magical when I get this message appear on my screen:

Whoohoo! Yipee! uh-huh, uh-huh! w00t! Yeah, baby!

(That's part of the message geochecker.com displays when you have entered the right coordinates for a puzzle geocache.)

And it's pretty magical when I spy a tough hide and I smile or yell, "found it!"

It's magical when I get over my (false) assumptions and get myself unstuck. Reminder to self whenever I am stuck (i.e., can't find something): what am I assuming? (Whatever it is, is usually the reason why I am stuck.)

It's magical walking through forests, spying deer and other wildlife, and feeling the energy of the forest.

Do you experience geocaching as being part of a community? If so, in what way(s)? Have people from the community become your friends?

Yes, yes. Practically all of my friends are geocachers. Sometimes I cache with them, sometimes alone. Sometimes I attend geocaching events.

What sorts of things do you pick up? What do you leave behind?

I pick up what I like. Often nothing. I like to find trackable geocoins—kinds that I haven't seen before. I leave behind something similar to what I take. We have signature Pycho Urban Cache buttons and magnets, so they are good to leave as trade items.

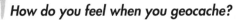

How do you feel when you geocache?

All sorts of different things. Frustrated (if I can't find the cache) happy, peaceful.

Vinny's Story

Sue's recent recounting of the tale of how we got involved in geocaching jibes with my memory as well. We live in a wilderness area in the mountains west of Frederick, Maryland, in a forested area crisscrossed with trails, most of them unnamed and unmarked. For several years, I had wistfully said that I wished that I had a cheap GPS receiver so that I could tell where I was with relation to home and to the roads as I followed some of these trails which twisted and turned through the dark and deep forest cover, but I would never have bothered to purchase a GPSr for myself.

Sue realized my wish for a GPSr but my reluctance to purchase one, and thus decided to give me one as a birthday present. And, since we live in deep forest, she did a lot of careful research online first to discover which GPS receivers worked best under deep forest cover, and decided after much research to purchase a Magellan SporTrak Pro. In hindsight, this turned out to have been a very wise decision, as the SporTrak proved itself to work very well even under deep forest cover, in contrast to many other brands and models of GPSrs on the market at that time.

After a few months, my own interest in finding most mainstream geocaches had waned, and I had found that I was specializing more and more only in finding and hiding extreme geocaches—that is, geocaches that involve extreme outdoor adventure in order to find them or to place them, many of which may require use of special equipment such as a boat, scuba gear, rock climbing gear or caving/spelunking gear, or even require the use of a helicopter or extremely complex technical equipment.

As of November 2006, our geocaching account has over 1,100 finds, and, as I point out on our profile page at Geocaching.com, Sue is solely responsible for the vast majority of those finds. I, on the other hand, have personally found perhaps only 250 of the finds listed for our joint account. However, due to fact that I do more long-distance travel (most of it for my scientific consulting work) than does Sue, I am responsible for our finds in distant states (i.e., California, Texas, Iowa, Wyoming, Wisconsin, etc.) and also for our cache find in Southern India and for a DNF log or two for caches in other countries (Germany and Nicaragua come to mind here).

I quickly lost interest in placing what I will call "ordinary" geo-caches in the woods, and instead found myself focusing more and more upon placing only what I will call "extreme terrain" geo-caches, where a seeker may need to use outdoor adventure skills and/or specialized gear in order to successfully find one of these geocaches. This eventually led to our Psycho Urban Cache series and to our smaller Psycho Backcountry Cache series, which, considering the fact that the majority of them are rather extreme terrain caches, have enjoyed quite a bit of popularity among some sectors of the geocaching community. These Psycho caches have been a lot of fun for me (and for Sue as well, for those in which she was involved) to place and it has also been a lot of fun to sit back and witness the level of interest created by some of these caches, and also to watch or to hear tales of the antics of those cachers who have gone after some of the more extreme of these caches.

Why do you geocache?

Why I geocache: because it is fun. And, for me, placing extreme geocaches is a way of saying "thank you" and giving something back to the geocaching community in general and also to the much smaller community of extreme geocachers. So, it is about fun and appreciation and gratitude.

Do you experience geocaching as being part of a community? If so, in what way(s)? Have people from the community become your friends?

Well, I tend to be a very private person, and thus I tend to deliberately limit the number of friends in my life. Having said that, I am very far from being an introvert, and I do love people and I love interacting with people in a wide variety of situations and settings, but I simply tend to strictly limit the amount of time which I spend doing so. This is largely because I find that I need lots of private time to really be able to listen well to what I will call my Heart and what I will call God and the angels, and to allow my Heart and God and the angels to guide my life. This is also why I choose to live in the wilderness in the mountains, as this helps to maintain my privacy. And, one of the hats which I wear in this life is that of a research and consulting scientist, and my own particular flavor on that is that I am definitely a very fun "mad scientist," and I have found that in order to be a good mad scientist, I need lots of private time, spent both in my lab and in prayer and mediation.

I must admit that despite my efforts to keep geocachers at a bit of a distance during the time I have been a geocacher, I have ended up making a number of good casual friends and acquaintances in the geocaching world. And I have even become a bit well-known in some odd circles and corners of the geocaching world—I suspect that a good part of that is simply due to the fact that I like to seek extreme geocaches, and also due to our rather well-known Psycho Urban Cache series.

I only tend to attend one or two geo-events per year, and when I do so, I am always amazed at the number of strangers who have heard of me and who know of me, and who approach me and want to talk with me. As I have hinted earlier, in addition to being a consulting scientist, I also have one foot in the spiritual world, and I am also amazed at the number of geocachers who have spent the time to research me and my identity a bit, and who discovered my spiritual side, and who then approach me at events wanting to talk about such non-geocaching interests. I find this fascinating and heartwarming.

SEVEN

Support

It is in community that we come to see God in the other.
It is in community that we see our own emptiness filled up.
It is community that calls me beyond the pinched horizons
of my own life, my own country, my own race, and
gives me the gifts I do not have within me.

—JOAN CHITTISTER (1936–)

I don't believe that there was ever a time in my life when I wasn't actively thinking about community.

I grew up going to parochial school, raised in a church that took the notion of community extremely seriously indeed. I was in my teens in the late sixties and early seventies, a heady time of passion and commitment that crystallized for me in the liberation theology movement. I read Gutiérrez and Helder Camara and Dorothee Sölle and Schillebeeckx and wrote long essays on social justice and poverty and the struggle for human rights.

I should note that it is no accident that I came to these writings and this inclination: I was a child of privilege, with a great deal of time and leisure to think philosophical thoughts—and enough mixed feelings about my advantages to rebel against them and ultimately make other choices for my life. As a homeless person later remarked to me, "Only people with money have time to think about things like that. The rest of us are busy just living." I have no doubt that there was a fair amount of guilt sprinkled in with my romanticism, but it still all created a powerful need to connect with and see myself as part of a community that was bigger than my immediate self, my immediate family, my immediate milieu. Something more important, more transcendent.

> Look for your passion and follow it, come what may, but do it from a Latino perspective, where you are guided by the effect of what you do on your family and your community. Being Latino is emotional, is spiritual, and to me it means moral structure: what is good, what is right, what is justice. All this will become more important as we go through some tough times ahead. We need to build on that. (David Hayes-Bautista)

I did come to believe, through—or perhaps in spite of—all my adolescent drama and romanticism, that community not only is the basis for all meaningful human interactions, but is also the only source of real self-actualization. Thinking about the world from the bottom up, so to speak, from the viewpoint of the poor and oppressed of the human community, I first learned the connections that I later made in poetry and literature, the truths of no man being an island and not asking for whom the bell tolls.

And I do believe that if humanity is to survive into the next century it will only be by caring for each other, by seeing that we really are in this together, and that all people are affected when one person is hurt. Community is not something that's an option anymore, if it ever even was one once. It's become the only means to survival.

> There is no such thing as a "self-made" man. We are made up of

thousands of others. Everyone who has ever done a kind deed for us, or spoken one word of encouragement to us, has entered into the make-up of our character and of our thoughts, as well as our success. *(George Matthew Adams)*

My friend Julie Blackburn and I have been close for so many years that it feels like forever. We're on the telephone at least once a day, sometimes more often, and there isn't much of anything that we haven't shared with each other. Recently she was talking about problems another friend was having with her partner. "It's all about connection, isn't it?" she asked rhetorically. "It's the only way we can manage to face everything, by having people you can count on to listen to you, to give you a different perspective on things."

This comment became visible—and graphic—when she and I went together to the funeral of a woman we'd both known, a young woman who had committed suicide the week before; the whole enterprise was unspeakably emotionally difficult. Cece had led a far too short and in many ways too intense life, and had alienated a fair number of people in the process; but the cemetery chapel was filled to overflowing with her friends, her people, her community who had all come to say goodbye.

After it was over—the funeral, the post-funeral gathering at a local pub, and hours at Julie's house spent talking about our mutual pasts—Julie said, "I thought I was really not going to be able to handle Cece's death. But going to the funeral . . . seeing all those people there . . . it really put things in perspective for me. She wasn't alone. That made all the difference."

And it does. That is, indeed, what makes all the difference. None of us is alone; we are surrounded by and sometimes supported by our community. We see it best in times of crisis; but wouldn't it be something to see it when we're *not* in need?

Years ago I recognized my kinship with all living things, and I made up my mind that I was not one bit better than the meanest on the earth. I said then and I say now, that while there is a lower class, I am in it; while there is a criminal element, I am of it; while there is a soul in prison, I am not free. *(Eugene Debs)*

I have belonged to one intentional community and have visited and studied others: Taizé, Iona, Plum Village. I have seen and experienced the struggle to live equitably, each giving according to his or her gifts, each receiving according to his or her needs.

It's not easy: as Richard Dawkins has pointed out, we are programmed to be selfish. We establish limits to our caring: myself, my family, my neighborhood, my country. Keep the circles as small as possible, so we don't have to share too much. I saw a man buy his son a car, but later that same day he couldn't be bothered to roll down the window of his SUV to hand a dollar bill to a homeless veteran.

We were taught under the old ethic that man's business on this earth was to look out for himself. That was the ethic of the jungle; the ethic of the wild beast. Take care of yourself, no matter what may become of your fellow man. Thousands of years ago the question was asked; "Am I my brother's keeper?" That question has never yet been answered in a way that is satisfactory to civilized society. Yes, I am my brother's keeper. I am under a moral obligation to him that is inspired, not by any maudlin sentimentality but by the higher duty I owe myself. What would you think me if I were capable of seating myself at a table and gorging myself with food and saw about me the children of my fellow beings starving to death? *(Eugene Debs)*

I was speaking with my friend Neil and happened to say to him, "You have to understand that my point of view is affected by the fact that I'm a Catholic and a socialist," to which he responded, "try not being anything for a while."

I laughed. "It's not in my nature," I said. "I love solitude, but I am defined by community."

"Your nature," Neil said, "is evolving."

We have all known the long loneliness and we have learned that the only solution is love and that love comes with community. (Dorothy Day)

While Neil and I will probably disagree forever about community, he did make a valid point: being part of and caring for the community does not mean losing oneself in it. To a certain extent I *am* defined by the groups to which I belong, and yet I am more than that. The human heart, the human soul, can never be encompassed by human conventions or associations—which, by their very being, are as incomplete and imperfect as the people who comprise them.

And the thought of incomplete and imperfect people brings us back to geocaching.

Yes, it's a community. A diverse, international, sometimes bizarre community of people drawn together because of their common interest in following a distant satellite's directions into the unknown.

I met my friend Claiborne Dawes (she goes by SearchingScribbler in the geocaching world) through geocaching, and even she (who is a *very* patient woman!) gets prickly about some geocachers, preferring other company when she goes into the woods: "As one who likes to stop and smell the flowers while geo-caching—to the occasional frustration of my most frequent caching partner—I recommend caching with grandchildren. They love treasure hunts, of course, and they are built lower to the ground! I remember my eldest granddaughter pointing out a little green snake from her three-foot vantage point; I would have missed it. I also loved watching her younger sister bounding fearlessly over rocks and roots last summer on our quest for a cache along a New Hampshire river. So find a child—almost any one will do—and head for the woods!"

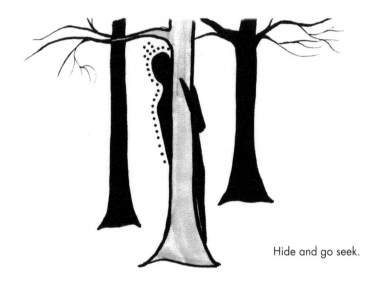

Hide and go seek.

But that, too, is part of the concept of community: learning to live with each other's habits, annoying or otherwise, and learning to recognize and do something about one's own. It's an ongoing process, a journey rather than a destination, this learning to live with each other. But it's worth it: it's well worth it.

And even those who call themselves individualists sometimes need help. Sometimes need the community. For them, and for all of us, the gathering-place is where it is for nearly every Internet-based community: in the online forums.

The Forums

Accessed through the geocaching.com site (click "forums" on the left side of the main page), the forums truly offer something for everybody, from people like me who can just about manage to read a GPS receiver to the most confirmed geeks around.

They are divided into nine main categories, most of which include a number of subcategories:

1. Groundspeak Notices—Geocaching Announcements

2. General Geocaching Discussions
   a. getting started
   b. geocaching topics
   c. geocaching.com website
   d. off-topic
   e. ache in, trash out
   f. geocaching chat

3. GPS-Related Topics
   a. GPS units and software
   b. GPS garage sale
   c. GPS in education
   d. benchmark hunting
   e. National Geodetic Survey
   f. National Map Corps
   g. GPS and ham radio

4. Geocaching Hitchhikers
   a. travel bugs
   b. geocoins

5. Geocaching Adventures
   a. The hunt/the unusual
   b. organized geocaching

6. Geocaching Groups by Region/State—Great Plains, Midwest, New England, Northeast, Northwest, South and Southeast, West and Southwest

7. Geocaching Groups by Country—All nations, Arabian peninsula, Australia, Belgium, Canada, French-speaking, German-speaking, Greece/Hellas, Italian-speaking, New Zealand, Nordic and Baltic countries, Portuguese-speaking, South Africa, South America, Spanish-speaking, United Kingdom.

8. Waymarking
   a. getting started with waymarking
   b. recruitment and category proposals
   c. waymark category discussion

9. Board Statistics
   a. users currently online
   b. forthcoming calendar events
   c. board statistics

So as you can see, there's the opportunity to talk about everything and nothing. You can play the usual online forum games—choose avatars to represent yourself, use emoticons in your speech, that sort of thing—and, while I haven't done it myself, I'm sure that there's the same level of flirting and posturing and so on happening here as happen in most online forums.

And there's gossip—ah, where would a community be without gossip? When I approached one of the people I wanted to interview for this book, his reaction was, "Yeah, I heard about you writing something."

Wow. Remind me never to share *secrets* online.

That's true, of course, of all communities, online or offline. It's part of the dark side of human nature, the *schadenfreude* that we feed on to reassure ourselves that we're really all right—after all, things could be worse, I could be *her*. And just as we slow down on the highway to stare in fascinated horror at other people's tragedies, so too in a less dramatic way we spread gossip about each other. "Did you *hear* . . .?"

Just as there's the expected sniping and backbiting in the geocaching community, though, there is also an experience that is warm and real and sometimes altogether unexpected. When a local geocacher died, the community rallied round his widow, who eventually came back to the hobby and touches her happiest memories of life with her husband that way.

There's also a great deal of genuine help and useful information on the forums, and that aspect of them should not be overlooked.

Want to find when the next CITO event in your area will be held? Want to express your frustration with a given map system (I'm not naming names!) or describe a close encounter with poison ivy? How about sharing pictures of you and your dog geocaching together? Are you concerned about encountering hunters in the woods? All these and many, many more topics are being explored on the forums as we speak.

Paul likes scanning the forums for clever hides and ideas for puzzles he may want to put together. I don't spend nearly the time on the forums that I should—not that there's any requirement to do so, but I often find amazing stories and interesting people there, and forget how much fun it can be when I haven't checked in for a few weeks.

The forums are very much what their name implies—the twenty-first-century, electronic version of the forums of the ancient world, places where people gathered and talked and transacted their business with each other and with the community at large.

There are times to be in the forums. There are times to be in the woods.

There is a time to be with your community, and there is a time to be alone with yourself.

Nature is always perfecting its balancing act. Too much of anything is a problem, and the earth always tries to recover balance as quickly as possible when there is an imbalance of any kind. We, too, are working that same balance beam, whether we know it or not. We juggle work and play, spirituality and sensuality, time apart and time together; we multitask to make sure we have time for the things we want to do and then we find ourselves multitasking through them, too.

But in our hearts we all are looking for that same balance. None of us is completely comfortable when we spend all our time with people, or all our time alone; it is the combination of community and solitude that makes a person whole.

What I suggest is that geocaching is an excellent vehicle for enabling that balance. Practicing the hobby will often involve other people—at events, on the forums, going out on caching runs together. It will also involve time alone, though, when no one in your family or among your friends "feels like" going with you—and your grumbling turns to peace as soon as you're in the woods. It's a magical transformation that amazes us every time it happens, and it happens every time we allow it to.

We've all heard the advice of the wise among us: everything in moderation. Perhaps if we substituted the word "balance" for "moderation" we'd be happier buying into the axiom: because it really is, in our hearts, what we all crave.

My commitment is to community. I am deeply involved in the peace movement because it is one of the things I can do for my community, even if my voice is ignored, even if I sometimes feel a little like Cassandra, seeing the future and having everyone disbelieve her. I do work for free for others who are caring for the community: nonprofits, volunteer organizations. I cannot live apart from my community: my chosen community of family and friends, my wider community of associates and colleagues, my still wider community of the world.

At the same time, when I go for too long without being alone, I start feeling sick. I start being unable to write, to feel, to express myself. I have organized my life around times of intense involvement in community and intense solitude, and it works. We don't all have my options, I know; and nor does everybody require the intensity of experience that I seem to need, the total immersion in one or the other.

But I repeat: to some extent, you need to find that balance in your life. You need to reflect nature in order to be part of it; and balance is the first step in that direction. You need the community and the community needs you, but you can only have something to give (and, indeed, something to receive) if you're able to assimilate these gifts in silence and solitude. Make sure to carve out some time doing just that.

Geocaching offers the perfect opportunity to explore that balance and to find where you are, what you need. And when it's time to carve out your times for silence, solitude, and meditation from your busy schedule, consider a trip into the woods with your GPS receiver.

Consider being apart so that you can appreciate yourself and so that you can appreciate your community. The woods are a wonderful place to take the time to examine all the issues you've been putting off thinking about. The woods are a wonderful place to find peace, and re-establish any balance between self and community that you feel might be missing in your life.

Thoreau found himself there. I'm convinced that you can, too.

A Conversation
with Brad Webb

"I was born in Delaware in 1942 and left there to go to college in Georgia in 1961. In 1964, I started my career with a technology company *and* got married, so that year is a big milestone in my life. My career took me to Ohio, New Hampshire, Connecticut, back to Delaware, South Carolina and Georgia. Business travel opportunities took me to Japan, Canada, Australia, Germany and The Netherlands, as well as to many of the larger cities in the United States. After retiring in 2004, we moved to the Lake Hartwell area of South Carolina from Georgia. My wife and I have two children and two grandchildren who we see often, as they live within an hour of our current location.

"My entry into geocaching came about due to a conversation between my wife and a neighbor's wife. The neighbor is a fairly avid outdoorsman who also participates in off-road adventures in his Land Rover, and he started geocaching as a related activity. This all took place back in the early months of 2001 when there were very few caches out there to be found. My interest in the sport came more from the technology side, and to get started I went out and got a GPS receiver just like his. Both of us are still using our Garmin GPS12MAP receivers quite effectively.

"Today geocaching is my primary hobby, with more of my time spent on reviewing new cache page submissions than anything else."

Why do you geocache?

Geocaching gives me a reason to get outside and go to places I ordinarily would not visit. I enjoy seeing the log entries of persons who have found caches that I have hidden.

What is your style of caching . . . how do you "play the game?"

I create very few caches, but when I do, I like to hide them in an unusual manner—not necessarily difficult, but unexpected. Since I am a volunteer reviewer for Groundspeak, I do not attempt to be FTF (unless the cache has been sitting there for a few days) and I usually do not do mystery or multistage caches.

The primary reason I take this approach is to avoid any perception that I am using information visible to me in an unfair manner. I do collect a few geocoins, but limit this to the coins of persons I know well and coins of the states where I review new cache pages for Groundspeak.

What is the most moving or magical thing that has happened to you when geocaching? Can you share that experience?

Some of the first geocaches I found, while generally unremarkable, are the ones that come most readily to mind. Finding the APE cache close to Atlanta was a big thing for me because all of my geocaching friends were in a frenzy to find it on the first day it became available.

(APE caches were part of a publicity effort to promote the 2001 remake of Planet of the Apes. Fox Studios placed a number of movie artifacts in caches, some of them becoming quite sought-after. You can read the whole story at markwell.us/project ape.htm)

Do you experience geocaching as being part of a community? If so, in what way(s)? Have people from the community become your friends?

I was a founding member of the Georgia Geocachers Association and a member of the original steering committee of the organization. This goes back to June of 2001, and in the early years geocachers were a closely knit group. Today, the sport of geocaching provides a common ground for persons meeting for the first time and provides an excellent opportunity to make new friends.

In my current role as a Groundspeak volunteer, I have several new friendships with geocachers in the New England and Delaware areas. When I have the opportunity to travel into these areas, it seems there is no end to the number of persons who go out of their way to treat me like an old friend. And of course I feel the same way toward those persons I have been interacting with through e-mail and other impersonal methods.

What sorts of things do you pick up? What do you leave behind?

I will sometimes pick up a travel bug if I can help it along toward its goal. I have ordered a batch of Pathtags, and once they arrive I will be leaving them in caches I visit as signature items. Other than that, I do little trading.

How do you feel when you geocache?

When searching for a cache, I feel a sense of adventure. Having said that, if you look at my finds, you will see that there are a fair number of easy micro caches in the list. But I still feel at least a small sense of adventure when I can look across a parking lot and guess which light pole has the skirt-lifter film canister hidden in it.

My wife is not particularly interested in geocaching, so I either go alone or leave her sitting in the car while I look for a cache. I really don't like leaving her sitting, so it is easier all around for me to focus on the easier caches.

How do you feel about you role as a Groundspeak volunteer, particularly in light of the scorn and abuse heaped on some volunteers in the Groundspeak forums?

My personal job description is to help geocachers get their cache pages published within the boundaries of the guidelines, and I believe most geocachers come to recognize that sooner rather than later. Before retirement, I spent 40 years in the customer services field, and I look at the geocachers I work with as my customers. It has been my experience that treating people in a respectful manner caused nearly all of them to treat me respectfully. I am very pleased with and proud of the rapport I have with the geocachers in the areas where I am the volunteer reviewer.

EIGHT

Okay, So I'll Give You a Few Nuts and Bolts After All

In Jewish tradition, one of the metaphors for God is the Tree of Life. We celebrate a midwinter festival that is the "new year for trees," when their life-juices stir once more and they begin to renew themselves from a wintry near-death. That festival is also understood as the "New Year of The Tree"-the time when God's abundance reawakens in the world. Since the forests are a direct expression of God's beauty, we must stir ourselves to save these forests now when they are dying in what could become a universal winter.

—RABBI ARTHUR WASKOW (CONTEMPORARY; BIRTHDATE UNKNOWN)

I said that I wouldn't, but I'd hate to leave you without going over some of the specifics that may have gotten lost while I was busy talking about hawks and dreams and Dorothy Day. So what I'm giving you here is a series of "cheat sheets"—feel free to clip them out and slip them into your backpack or put them next to your computer as quick references. For more in-depth information on any of these topics, consult one of the books or websites listed in the *Resources* section in the back of the book . . . or, indeed, the geo-caching.com site itself.

Finding a cache: the cheat sheet

Okay, so you want to find a cache. Here's what you really need to know:

1. Go to geocaching.com and click "Hide and Seek a Cache" in the menu on the left side of the page.

2. The page that will be returned is titled "Tools for Finding and Hiding Caches." On the left side of the page is an option for entering your zip code to locate caches near you.

3. Find a cache that sounds interesting. Make sure that it is not a micro (really difficult to find if you don't have experience) or a puzzle (really difficult to find—for very different reasons!—if you don't have experience).

4. Put the cache coordinates into your GPS unit following the directions in the unit's owner's manual. Note: you may wish to have another person check and make sure that they were entered correctly. At one time or another, everyone has made errors entering coordinates, and ended up very far away indeed from where they want to be. Don't let that happen to you the first time out!

5. Now click the Google maps link from the cache page to get close to the cache and see approximately where it's located.

6. Print out the cache page to take with you. A lot of people like to store and work caches from their PDAs, but you may need to decrypt the clue, and some people find it easier to do on paper (though caching software written for the PDA will also do it for you) .

7. Gather up your stuff—we did talk about what you should carry with you every time you go out in an earlier chapter, didn't we?—and you're off!

Placing a cache: the cheat sheet

Start by doing some research into a nearby area that appears promising, or you may already have a favorite place you'd like people to see and enjoy. Bear in mind the cardinal rules of cache placement: Do not place near any infrastructures such as a bridge, a water tower, an airport, a tunnel, etc., or any federal or state building; your cache could be misinterpreted. Do not place near a school or any building used for religious meetings. Do not place on private land without the landowner's permission. Check and be sure if you have any question as to whether geocaching is permitted in a given place—some federal and state agencies allow it, some do not. Do not place it in an environmental or cultural protected area. Don't place it within 500 feet of another cache.

Now that you know where you *can't* place a cache, find a location that you like and go for it.

1. Get a waterproof container and fill it with small treasures (Tupperware and Gladware do not remain waterproof; use Lock-and-Lock or Snapware instead). If you've decided to have a signature item, you can include it. Include something that identifies it as a geocache (this is mostly for the benefit of muggles); sample information sheets are available on the geocaching.com site. Also include a logbook and several pens or pencils; it's advisable to place these in a sealed plastic bag.

2. Hide the geocache! Be tricky. Be clever. Walk away from it when you've finished and look back and see if anything points to its location.

3. Record the location with your GPSr. Take several readings to get one that is accurate; the unit will take an average for you. Some receivers will automatically average; check into this when you purchase a unit.

Submitting a cache: the cheat sheet

1. When you've placed your cache and taken GPS readings, go to geocaching.com and click *Hide and Seek a Cache.*

2. On the right side of the screen is the section for hiding a cache. Click the link that says *Fill Out Our Online Form.*

3. The returned page will ask you to make some choices from pull-down menus. The cache type should be obvious (see chapter one if you have any questions), as is the cache size. Choose a nickname for the cache, and your name for placing the cache (only one person may place a cache, which is why Paul and I alternate who "places" our Bread & Roses geo-events).

4. Check that the cache is active (you may later choose to archive it, but for now you want it to be active).

5. Date.

6. Related web page: ignore unless you have a related website.

7. Now's the time to check and double-check your work: it's embarrassing and awkward to send people to the wrong place! Use the drop-down list and text entry boxes to enter the cache coordinates

8. Fill in the location from the boxes.

9. You have to rate the difficulty of the cache itself and, separately, the difficulty of the terrain. The best way to get a feel for the ratings is to find some caches and read their ratings to see how others have evaluated difficulty and terrain; the online guide is also an excellent information source here.

10. If you know HTML and want to use it, you have that option here.

11. Descriptions: the short one is the sentence or two that people will probably read to see if they want to find out more about your cache; the long one is where you go into detail. Again, read others' descriptions to see what makes sense for your cache. Save your long description on your computer in a file; that way, if something goes wrong, you don't have to do the hard part all over again!

12. You can leave a hint for frustrated cachers in the next section; it's encrypted so that people can try first.

13. If you need to tell the cache approver anything, enter it as a *Note to reviewer* here.

14. Click the legal disclaimer that you're used to clicking on just about every website you visit.

15. Click *Report New Listing,* and you're done!

Maintaining a cache: the cheat sheet

Your cache is your responsibility: it needs attention. In general, if you read people's logs for your cache (you can do this by clicking the *Watch This Cache* button at the top of the cache information page), you'll have a sense of how things are going. But you'll also want to visit it on a regular basis: check the logbook (may need replacing), the pens and pencils (replace or sharpen as needed), and of course the trinkets may need thinning or restocking.

It probably won't happen, but should anyone log a comment that is inappropriate in content (abusive, angry, or giving away too much information) you have the right—and, indeed, the responsibility—to moderate or remove those comments.

That's It for the Cheat Sheets

Again, I refer you to the resource section in the back of this book so that you can go beyond this simple nuts-and-bolts whirlwind tour of the specifics of geocaching. There will always be more to be learned—I became acutely aware of that fact as I prepared to write this book—and more ways to explore and refine your skills as you acquire them. Start with a good understanding of the basics, however, and you'll be able to appropriate what you need from the hobby in order to open your heart.

The more you understand geocaching's basic philosophy and guidelines, the more you'll be able to answer the question that I posed to all the people with whom I had conversations to place in this book: How do *you* play the game?

I'll make a brief confession here: this isn't how I did it. I knew about geocaching.com, of course, and dutifully logged my caches and travel bugs and so on. I never read any of the books, though, and only learned about the nuts and bolts as I had to. . . I'd say, as I was forced to by circumstances. Most people who know me find it supremely ironic that I once earned a living as a technical writer in view of the fact that I have great difficulty reading instructions. This stems, of course, from the fact that I really, really hate being told what to do. In any case, I don't read manuals, and I certainly wasn't going to waste time reading anything instructional when it came to geocaching. My heart was way out in front of me on this one: I wanted to be out there doing it, not in here reading about it.

And that is pretty much how I've done it. I learn what I need to know when I need to know it. It means I don't have a very good repertoire from which to draw when something new presents itself; I'm not necessarily prescribing my method as the best one out there. I just wanted to be in the woods, with the morning sun slant-

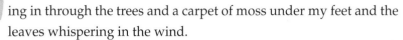

ing in through the trees and a carpet of moss under my feet and the leaves whispering in the wind.

In fact, I never read any of the books on geocaching until I needed to read them so that they could be included in my own resources section.

So—perhaps what I'm saying is, do as I say and not as I do. On the other hand, my heart has been opened through geocaching. I think that perhaps yours could be, too.

Whether you read the manuals or not.

What about a GPS receiver?

Okay. Here's the best advice I can give you. When looking for a GPS receiver, go either for the bottom or the top.

If you're not sure that you're going to like geocaching, don't make a purchase you'll later regret. People upgrade their GPS receivers all the time, so it's quite easy to find one at a yard sale or on a local Craigslist for around thirty-five dollars. Buy it, no matter what brand, and see if this is something you'll want to do more than once.

Otherwise, go for the best. Buy one that does auto-routing and buy good maps (available as downloadable software) for it. The Magellans do this and they hold signal well in the woods. If you want a Garmin, you'll want one of the ones with the SiRF chip.

There isn't much point that I see in buying anything in the middle ground—you'll have more frustration than fun.

And Now for Something Completely Different

Don't let the nuts-and-bolts of this chapter discourage you from finding a deeper meaning behind all the treasure hunting.

Stay with me here: let's assume that you *do* want to go out "there" and that finding a geocache sounds like a pleasant excuse, or destination, or incentive. Whichever works for you is fine with me.

So you're in the woods. Perhaps you've found your first geocache, you've signed the logbook, you've done a trinket exchange, you've danced the happy dance. Now what?

Now, if I may make a suggestion, don't do anything.

Remember this: you were drawn to this place because someone (the person who placed the cache) thought it was an important place. That person wanted to share it with you, and of all the geocaches you could have chosen as your first one, you chose this one. There must be something here for you, if you can only take the time to discover it.

So let's find out what it is.

Start by staying still, or as still as your restless body will allow you to be. *Breathe.* Breathe consciously, being aware of the breath entering your body, being held there, being released. Push it out, all the stale air trapped in the bottom of your diaphragm; let it out into this place, and take in the magical air instead.

Breathe.

As you breathe, feel yourself incorporating the space that surrounds you: take its air into you, let it become part of you. *Breathe.* As you release the breath, let yourself become part of the space you are in. You are part of it and it is part of you: you are an organic whole, your being flowing into the place and the place flowing into your being. *Breathe.*

Breathe.

Now sit down, if you're in a place where you can. Do it slowly, still feeling your connection to the space you are in. Breathe deeply, consciously. Close your eyes. Focus on your breathing: taking in the forest smells, letting out whatever anxieties are still clustered inside you.

Now start to explore, still with your eyes closed, the place where you are sitting. What do you hear? Can you isolate the different sounds, wind rustling the leaves in the trees, animals in the underbrush, the whine of insects, birds—all the different birds—surrounding you?

Feel the air against your skin. How is it different from the air in your home, in your car, at your workplace? *Breathe.*

Open your eyes, slowly, gradually. Look around you. Touch the ground or the rock or the fallen tree beneath you. Feel this place that you're in. *Breathe.*

You were brought here because there was something here for you to find. What is it? Have you seen what the cache hider meant for you to see? Has it touched you?

Stretch, reaching as high above your head as you can. Release. *Breathe.*

When you're ready, you can stand up. Try and carry this place with you as you leave: now that you have been here, it is part of you forever, just as you are part of it. If you see rubbish around you, take it: this is *your* space, now—you've touched it and it's touched you—and you want it to be beautiful.

And . . . *breathe.*

A Conversation with Jacob Czarnecki

Jacob Czarnecki is known in the geocaching world as "NotYour-Name." He's a fourteen-year-old geocacher—and the author's stepson. Besides going geocaching, he spends his free time listening to music, as well as playing and writing it. He is in two local bands and plays bass in both. He also likes to read, mostly Dean Koontz, Dennis Lehane, and Phil Rickman. He's been geocaching for about two years.

Why do you geocache?

I geocache for many reasons. Without geocaching, a lot of areas that are really interesting would be unknown to me. When someone sends you out into the woods, or to a spot that is important to them, you are almost always going somewhere new. That in itself is fairly rewarding, and then of course so is finding the cache. Through geocaching, you can experience nature, meet new people, learn things about certain areas (be it a city or in the woods) and of course, get some exercise.

What is your style of caching—how do you "play the game"?

I would say I play the game in a couple of ways. I really like to go out and walk through the woods, or through an interesting area in the city. I like some caches where one can learn, like the cache in Manchester in which you go to a lot of mill-related sites. Also, there is an element of competition. I like going out on first-to-find runs. This basically entails getting up before the crack of dawn and going out to a newly published cache that no one has yet found. When you get to the woods, the sun is starting to rise. You have the privilege of being the first people go find it, and of course, when you have beat out all the other people trying to get it, that's great, too.

What is the most moving or magical thing that has happened to you when geocaching? Can you share that experience?

I think one of my best geocaching experiences was on probably the second cache we did as a family. It was in an old military base in New Hampshire. It was nice to see all the vacated buildings, and to wonder what everything was once used for, and to imagine it as a bustling military establishment.

Do you experience geocaching as being part of a community? If so, in what way(s)? Have people from the community become your friends?

I do think that geocaching is a community, in ways. Since not too many people do it, you all have the common bond of being part of a larger thing that many people have never heard of. You all have some common interests, be it solving difficult puzzles, hiking through the woods, or learning about a city through a sport. I have become friends with some people through the geocaching community.

What sorts of things do you pick up? What do you leave behind?

Normally, I don't trade items, but when I do, normally it is a special FTF prize or an item which I find interesting. Some prizes I've gotten were pens, and travel bug dog tags. I've also known people to leave gift cards and geocoins as prizes. I do enjoy taking travel bugs, as well as geocoins. When I leave items, they're generally a travel bug, a geocoin, or a little Hot Wheels car.

How do you feel when you geocache?

When I geocache, I'm generally calm. I mean, you're walking through the woods, which in themselves are a very peaceful environment, and you're out to find something. You also to try and leave as small a print as you can on the woods. Sometimes, you lessen other people's prints by collecting trash or other debris just lying around from people who didn't really care about the environment .

What question am I forgetting to ask that you'd like to answer?

I guess a question you could have asked me would have been, "Do you think that you will be geocaching in X amount of years?" My answer, unless X was to equal some fantastically huge number, would be yes. I see no real reason to stop. It's a great sport, and it introduces me to new people and places. I love getting out in the woods, and to see spots that are important to people, and to learn about things that interest them, or things that they think it is important to know. So, unless there is a tragic accident involving my legs and a giant whirling blade, I do intend to keep geocaching. And if that accident does occur, I'll still try and hit urban caches.

NINE

What Else Is There?

Reading about nature is fine, but if a person walks in the
woods and listens carefully, he can learn more than what
is in books, for they speak with the voice of God.

GEORGE WASHINGTON CARVER (1864–1943)

There are a number of activities that can be seen as predeces-
sors or offshoots of geocaching, or just as allied activities.
Some of them can even be combined with geocaching (letterboxing, doing bookcrossing, and benchmarking come immediately to
mind). Some people have mentioned the conflict that ensues
when a spouse or partner doesn't enjoy geocaching; if you're one
of these people, you might just get lucky and hit on something
here that your significant other likes and that can be combined
with your geocaching—so that you end up with something for
both of you.

There are activities that are less organized than geocaching and
activities that are more so. Some of these activities are well known;
others are more obscure. All of them give you the opportunity to
explore the world in some way or another—by finding hidden
treasures in the woods, by passing on and discovering new books,

by learning the planet through maps, by getting back to the basics of using a compass and taking bearings from control-points.

In each of these activities, you can find a way to explore the world around you . . . and the world inside you.

And the explorations are not so very different from each other.

I love maps. Before I got married, on "free" days I used to pull out a map of New England, close my eyes, and stick a pin in the map: that became my destination, the end-point of my field trip. The more obscure the place, the better. I got in my car and explored places I'd never have thought to go on my own, and discovered wonderful, mundane, bizarre, and surprising experiences.

With my family of origin, as well as with my family of choice, I've always played word games. One of them is "geography," a game in which one must name as many places as possible, sometimes using the same starting letter, sometimes using the last letter of the preceding place-name. When I was a child, preparation for these games always involved a quick and furtive visit to an atlas or a globe in a last desperate attempt to cram even more geographic locations into my mind.

It never worked, of course.

Places, and especially new places, have always held tremendous fascination for me—and I suspect that if you're reading this, they might hold that same fascination for you. Exploring places with an interesting history, exploring places that inspire stories: these are explorations that open the heart and feed the soul.

While geocaching brings you to a very specific very local place to explore, you can start out your quest with a bird's-eye view— through maps.

Several of the activities below will inspire you to learn more about maps and how to use them. And even if you don't fall in love with the activity, I'd like to suggest that you make an effort to learn something about maps in general, and topographic maps in particular. It will enrich your wilderness experience—and could well save your life.

Letterboxes

As mentioned at the beginning of this book, letterboxes are in many ways the parents of today's geocaches. Letterboxing started in England over a century ago—and may well have itself been an outgrowth of the habit of leaving letters in tree hollows or other natural mailboxes. The game remains more popular in England (there may be 50,000 of them hidden) than in the United States (where the number is closer to between 5,000 and 10,000).

The description on the letterboxing site reads:

> Letterboxing is an intriguing mix of treasure hunting, art, navigation, and exploring interesting, scenic, and sometimes remote places. It takes the ancient custom of placing a rock on a cairn upon reaching the summit of a mountain to an artform. It started when a gentleman simply left his calling card in a bottle by a remote pool on the moors of Dartmoor, in England.
>
> Here's the basic idea: Someone hides a waterproof box somewhere (in a beautiful, interesting, or remote location) containing at least a logbook and a carved rubber stamp, and perhaps other goodies. The hider then usually writes directions to the box (called "clues" or "the map"), which can be straightforward, cryptic, or any degree in between. Often the clues involve map coordinates or compass bearings from landmarks, but they don't have to. Selecting a location and writing the clues is one aspect of the art.

Modern letterboxes are hidden in much the same manner as geocaches. Like geocaches, they contain logbooks. Instead of trinkets and hitchhikers, they contain a rubber stamp that is specific to that letterbox, as well as an inkpad.

Letterboxers themselves carry those same articles: small notebooks and a rubber stamp. While the stamp in the letterbox is specific to that letterbox, the ones carried by letterboxers are unique to that person—and can sometimes be very beautiful and very elaborate.

Some have made a rule that the letterboxer's stamp must be his or her own creation, though for the artistically challenged among us, this can be difficult or impossible. Paul (who is not artistically challenged) made mine. If he hadn't made it, I was going to go with an old typeface I had with my initial surrounded by flowers and swirls and who knows what else, and to hell with the rule. It's a nice rule made by somebody who has absolutely no idea how frustrated those of us who cannot transfer our feelings onto some concrete medium can become!

The practice is to find the letterbox and place one's stamp in the letterbox log, while using the letterbox stamp in one's own notebook (somewhat along the lines of stamps in a passport). Collecting the different and unusual stamps is really more delightful than I had anticipated; like geocaching, letterboxing often draws you into the woods, by streams, to places of serene beauty you might never have seen otherwise.

For more information on letterboxing, and to explore whether it might be a place where you can find your joy, check it out at letterboxing.org.

Benchmarking

Benchmarks are markers (usually metal) placed by the National Geodetic Survey—a government agency—in structures, rocks, concrete . . . in other words, in things that are not likely to move, change, or be destroyed. Benchmarks are used by surveyors, engineers, cartographers and other officials as control points so that bearings can be taken from them.

Benchmarks generally fall into two categories: **vertical control points** meant to establish the elevation of that particular point (usually a small brass or aluminum disc or a concrete post or iron pin) and **horizontal control points** meant to establish the coordinates of the point (again, usually a small brass or aluminum disc, though horizontal control points can also be edifices such as water towers or church spires; they can even be the tops of mountains—anyplace that can be seen from a distance. In this case, the object *is* the benchmark). Surveyors only call the vertical control points benchmarks, but in geocaching the term applies to both vertical and horizontal control points.

You can find and record benchmarks at the geocaching.com website. Go to the main page and you'll see that the third option on the left-hand menu is *Find a Benchmark.* Here you'll find information about benchmarks, how to find one (a process that simply involves placing your zip code in a search field; the website returns the results), and what the search is like.

When we talk about the search, we're talking about something that is probably best described as being midway between geocaching and letterboxing, in that you want to use your GPS receiver to get to the general area, then use the directions you printed out from the site to actually find it. Many if not most of the benchmarks were put in place "the old-fashioned way," to quote an old ad tagline; the coordinates were determined by using a ruler on a paper topographic map. Some of the coordinates are therefore not as accurate as they would have been had the GPS been available to those surveyors, and they depended on references to nearby objects to point to the benchmark. (On the other hand, the vertical coordinates, which are the only ones used by surveyors anyway, are in fact dead-on, since the whole point of the benchmark is to provide an accurate elevation marker for mapping and construction purposes.)

I have to say that I *like* the fact that you have to follow directions:

doing so ensures that you really look at what's around you ("There is a small group of trees near the water. Beyond that are two large rocks. . ."); I've seen way too many people standing in the middle of the hushed cathedral of a forest, their heads bent over their GPS units, seeing nothing; this doesn't allow you to do that.

Look up.

The geocaching site also cross-references geocaches and benchmarks, so you can find them both in one outing if you'd like. It makes for a change in the routine of looking for ammo cans or plastic boxes, and it's rather exciting to think about the people who placed that marker there. The date is always visible, and it's amazing to imagine how the world in general—and this little corner of it in particular—looked to the surveyors then.

The other side to that mental meandering, of course, is that the surveyors were there in the first place because someone had decided that this land should be owned and used, perhaps even parceled out and built upon. It may be a fact of modern life, but it's worth a few minutes of reflection. First Nations tribes believed that the land could not be owned; there is some wisdom in that worldview.

You can also check out benchmarks at the National Geodetic Survey at ngs.noaa.gov if you'd like to go to the source, though the site is not easy to navigate and the datasheets not particularly user-friendly.

Waymarking

Waymarking (the site is also run by Groundspeak) is essentially what virtual geocaches used to be: a way to mark (check out the name!) certain places or things so that others may visit them and be enriched by the experience.

From the waymarking site: "Waymarking is a way to mark unique locations on the planet and give them a voice. While GPS technology allows us to pinpoint any location on the planet, mark the location, and share it with others, Waymarking is the toolset for categorizing and adding unique information for that location. Groundspeak's slogan is *The Language of Location* and our goal is to give people the tools to help others share and discover unique and interesting locations on the planet. We invite you to share your part of the world with us through waymarking.com."

A waymark is a location that contains unique information defined within a theme, called a waymark category. Each waymark category has specific submission requirements and content.

Your login information from the geocaching site works on the waymarking site as well, since both belong to Groundspeak. As is true with the geocaching site, users have personal pages and statistics on the waymarking site. There are no forums for discussion, but there is a waymarking section in the geocaching site's forums; in some ways one can think of the waymarking site as an extension of the geocaching one.

Will you open your heart with waymarking? It's a very tempting proposition, in view of the fact that the lack of race to a treasure may mean that for waymarkers, the journey is the purpose. And while finding the location is important, the location itself needs to be striking enough to warrant the search—people do try to make them memorable (though it has to be said that the first waymark was a McDonald's fast-food restaurant—probably not the most scenic spot on earth!).

It's easy to see how many people who are less competitive and more contemplative enjoy waymarking over geocaching. You may find that you do, too.

Orienteering

Now that you've learned about geocaching, the description of orienteering is going to sound eerily familiar: it's a competitive form of land navigation.

(Okay, so it's not familiar if you plan to geocache the way I do, *sans* competition, but I know a lot of geocachers who might think that you'd just described geocaching.)

Orienteering participants must locate control points (like waypoints) by using a map and compass (no GPS units allowed here!) for navigation.

Orienteering began in Scandinavia in the nineteenth century as a part of standard military training; it's clearly useful for troops to be able to find their way into—and, perhaps more importantly, out of—the woods. In 1919 a Swede named Ernst Killander decided to make it into a civilian sport as well; then, in the early thirties, the brothers Kjellstron (Alvan and Bjorn to be exact, should the question ever come up in *Trivial Pursuit: The Obscure Edition*) invented a fast and precise new compass and suddenly everyone wanted to go orienteering.

As the sport is practiced today, it's a combination of mental acuity and physical skills that can prove, or so I am told, quite addictive. Speed is less important than being able to think quickly, register and process new information, and perform under pressure.

Orienteers are given a 1:50,000 topographic map with the various control points circled. Each point has a flag marker and a distinctive punch that is used to mark the orienteer's scorecard, which is carried with him or her. Competitive orienteering involves *running* from checkpoint to checkpoint—though, again, this is less a matter of speed than it is of getting there more quickly than others, not as oxymoronic a proposition as it sounds. Remember the tortoise and the hare?

Orienteering, unlike geocaching, *always* takes place in the woods. Orienteers are urged not to use their compasses to orient their maps. Instead, they rely on a number of orienteering techniques, which include:

- **pacing** (keeping track of distance covered when walking and running)

- **thumbing** (no, not hitchhiking, though that's what my generation called it. This is more serious: putting your thumb next to your location on a folded map; you then move from point to point on the ground without moving your thumb from its location. The thumb is then used as a point of reference for your last location in order to figure out your current one.)

- **handrails** (using existing linear features—fences, roads, streams—plotted along the route in order to move quickly)

- **attack points** (permanent known landmarks, like bridges and road intersections; the name is clearly a leftover from orienteering's military past)

There are presently around seventy orienteering clubs in the United States. Orienteering has expanded and the International Orienteering Federation now recognizes orienteering on foot, on mountain bicycles, and on skis; there's also something called trail orienteering that offers people with limited mobility the opportunity to participate in the sport as well.

To learn more and see whether this is a way you'd like to open your heart, check it out at orienteering.org.

Degree Confluence Project

The Degree Confluence Project's goal is to visit each of the latitude and longitude integer degree intersections in the world and take photographs at each location. Pictures, and the stories surrounding them, are posted at the project's website.

The project began in 1996 because its originator, Alex Jarrett, "liked the idea of visiting a location represented by a round number such as 43° 00'00"N, 72° 00'00"W. What would be there? Would other people have recognized it as a unique spot?" He wanted to give people a reason to get outside, move around a little, and record their activity. Sounds a little like . . . um . . . geocaching!

As of this writing there are 4782 primary confluences, 441 secondary confluences, and 309 incomplete confluences recorded. When asked why they participated in the Degree Confluence Project, people begin sounding a lot like geocachers: they wanted to go somewhere they hadn't been before, to visit places that tourists don't visit, to challenge what our society and our culture tell us is important. They like the thrill of the hunt and of the unknown, the sense of being embraced by a place, of meeting the people who live locally.

Want to travel and help? You, too, can participate. There are directions on the website for visiting a confluence and submitting a visit to the project.

Want to learn more about geography in a way your teachers at school never envisioned? All you have to do is visit the website and immerse yourself in the photographs. They'll give you a stark but amazing view of the earth as pieced together one bit at a time.

As a writer, I was naturally more interested in the stories attached to some parts of the project. I think that as a reader, you might be, too. I was spellbound at the description of months spent traveling around rural China to visit and record nineteen confluences. It's as good a reason to travel as any, and better than most.

To learn more about opening your heart through the Degree Confluence Project, visit them at confluence.org.

Armchair Treasure Hunt Club

Speaking of armchairs, if you're not up for the great outdoors, why not try the Armchair Treasure Hunt Club? I have to admit: If I lived in Great Britain, I'd join, in a heartbeat. I may, anyway, just to read and try to solve the puzzles!

Many years ago, when I first started offering freelance writing/editing/research work (before the ease of the Internet, when one actually advertised in newspapers), I had a client who researched and subsequently searched for and dived sunken ships. He wasn't doing it for archaeological research; he was doing it to get rich. I was employed to look through the "ships sighted" logs in public and private collections in New England; this information was helpful in pinpointing wreck sites. And even though I was only doing a small part of the research, it was one of the most exciting projects I ever did, with the promise that I might be able to participate in some way on the actual dive should one of "my" ships be located. And can I tell you how exciting that was, even participating to that

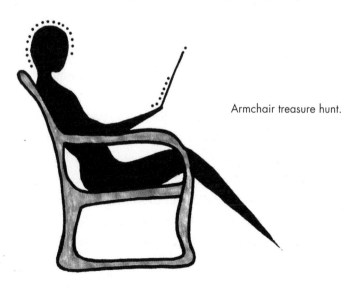

Armchair treasure hunt.

small extent in a real treasure hunt? I was looking for where "x marks the spot"—how cool is that?

Later, doing research for a book of my own, I came across the stories of the pirate Peter Eastman and the promises of his own treasure, put aside for his old age, in Newfoundland. And again there was that *frisson* of excitement, that sense of delight at the prospect of seeking and finding . . . *buried treasure!*

There is perhaps a part of all of us that wants to be Indiana Jones, to travel to exotic places and discover hidden treasure. Well, most of us can't; in fact, the "exotic places" is, for most of us, beyond our reach. But if you live in the United Kingdom, or visit there frequently, you can become part of a hunt and discovery of not-so-ancient buried treasure with clues that can be solved from the comfort of your armchair, kitchen table, bed . . . whatever works for you.

The Armchair Hunt Club produces treasure hunts that offer the opportunity for club members to try and outwit each other (in this case, first-to-find is also only-to-find!) in the search for buried or otherwise hidden treasure. Founded in 1992, the club produces a monthly newsletter with the current hunt (as well as past unsolved hunts) included, as well as other items of interest to members.

From treasureclub.net: "The first Club Treasure Hunt (March 1992) written and produced by Dan James himself was entitled *A Timeless Moral*. The prize, a statuette of the character within the story, Dr Emmanuel Worsfold,, was crafted in bronze, and set on a rosewood base embellished with silver decorations, beaten, cut, and polished by hand. This treasure remained buried for three years, as people from all walks of life tried to solve the hidden clues within the story."

You have to admit that sounds like a lot of fun! Very different from geocaching, but with an old-fashioned sort of aura that I think is rather delightful. If you plan on being in Great Britain in the near future, consider becoming a member and trying your hand at it! Learn more and perhaps decide to open your heart through the Armchair Treasure Hunt Club at treasurehunt.net.

Bookcrossing

Remember my story about travel bugs? The one where I talked about not letting one's ego get involved and expect others to behave as one wants them to? I should have already learned that particular lesson. In my experience, before there was the *Little Lamb* travel bug, there was Bookcrossing.

I found my first Bookcrossing book on a sunny Sunday afternoon in Provincetown, walking down Commercial Street with Paul after a service at the Unitarian-Universalist Meeting House. And there it was, sitting in the sun, just waiting for me: a hardcover copy of Barbara Kingsolver's *Prodigal Summer*. A brilliant book, well written, absorbing, filled with ideas that last long after the last page has been finished.

And what a concept! Finish reading a book, send it out into the wild, track its travels. See how a wonderful book can touch others' lives, awake others' minds! I was excited. I was beside myself.

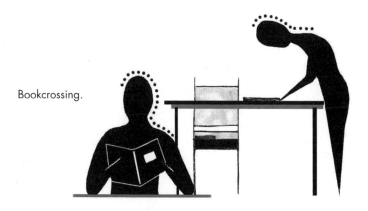

Bookcrossing.

I went to the website and printed out any number of Bookcrossing stickers, and thinned out my own library. (Well, okay, thinned it out *slightly*.) I started traveling with books, and started looking at various locations in light of their being potential Bookcrossing drops. I left my books everywhere: at bus stops, in parks, on benches, in museums, in hospital waiting rooms. I sent them out into the world, and waited with happy anticipation for news of their travels.

Like geocaching travel bugs, Bookcrossing books can be logged as having been found, reactions to the book posted to the website, and the new drop-off point noted. My Kingsolver book had been all over the country before ending up in Provincetown; and I, myself, passed it along in Boston. What fun!

Except that no one was logging my books.

Not only was no one logging my books, I went back and scrutinized the places where I'd left them off. Zip. They were gone; and as time passed it became abundantly clear that not only were they not being logged, they weren't *going* to be logged.

Shades of *Little Lamb, Who Made Thee*!

It was Paul who was, once again, the voice of steadying wisdom in the midst of my spinning emotions. "Look at it this way," he said reasonably. "You're sending the books out so that they can be read. Someone's obviously reading them. So you got what you wanted."

Well—almost.

He caught my expression. "But you really wanted to read the logs," he said, his voice gentle.

I nodded. "I really wanted to read the logs," I concurred glumly.

"I guess," Paul said carefully, "That you're going to have to decide where your joy comes from—sharing your books or having people tell you how much they appreciate you for sharing them."

Have I mentioned that he has a way of cutting through layers of nonsense to get to the core of a question?

That really is the core of this or any question, though, and it goes to the center of this series of books. What else could opening your heart be but a way of finding where your joy comes from?

Open your heart . . . find your joy.

Bookcrossing is a wonderful way of exploring, particularly when you read logs (not necessarily those of your own books!). You can read, and share what you're reading. You can explore new authors through other people sharing their joy with you. You can follow the progress of a given book—all without leaving your favorite chair. It's a great place to find your joy.

It's clear from the number of Bookcrossing books finding their way into caches that many people find the two activities compatible, and the next time you go geocaching you may want to slip a paperback in the cache you discover as well. Go to bookcrossing. com and log your book; print out a sticker and put it in the book (I just use transparent tape, though you can buy fancy stickers on the bookcrossing site); and log it into the cache. Voilà!

Want the history? From the Bookcrossing.com site: "BookCrossing.com is a labor of love that was conceived and is maintained by Humankind Systems, a software and internet development company with offices in Kansas City, Missouri, and Sandpoint, Idaho. Looking for a break from the doldrums of creating yet another e-commerce website (that's just what the world needs), or email server application (oooh, those are doubly exciting), Humankind partner BookCrossings sought to create a community site that would be the first of its kind, that would give back to the world at large, and that would provide warm fuzzy feelings whenever he worked on it. BookCrossing.com was the result."

So go and try it out!

And keep looking for the places where you find *your* joy. You'll be amazed at how many there are.

A Word in Parting

There is magic everywhere.

I grew up finding it in a place where many people would expect it precisely not to be: in a Roman Catholic convent school. We got up early—*very* early—and were at Mass first thing, while it was still dark outside. And surrounded by that darkness, our community— sisters and students alike—gathered, a community at one. And we lit candles against the darkness and we burned incense and we sang, long, haunting, wandering chants that spoke so eloquently of our own wandering spirits. And we prayed.

And somewhere in that mixture, magic happened. Was it because all of our senses were so powerfully called together— remember how I said, earlier, that all spirituality is by its very nature, against all expectations and assumptions, incarnational— with the fire and the smells and the sounds and the feelings all coming together to create something that took on a life of its own, that was called into being by our energy? or was it something simpler than that—the magic of being awake before the rest of the world (or so it seemed to me, then), praying with all our hearts for people we would never meet, who would never know that we were praying for them?

I don't know what made the magic; I only know that it was there.

Magic surrounds you even now as you read this. My energy, your energy, the energy that is all around you, they're all creating something new and different in this very moment, something that never existed before. Reach out and touch that magic; lay claim to it as your own.

Listen to your dreams.

Look up.

Breathe.

Follow your joy.

And if geocaching can open your heart, welcome to it. If another activity in this book seems more likely to open your heart, then do go and pursue it. There is joy to be found everywhere, magic to be found everywhere, and opening your heart is the first and continuous step toward accessing it all.

As I was putting the final touches on this book—after, in fact, it had already gone to the publisher—I received this note about the *Dark Satanic Mills* cache:

> I LOVED this cache. It did what this hobby is meant to do—changed my perspective. Stage Four was sad, but the waypoint itself was well chosen, and brought back a flood of memories from childhood, including a cardigan sweater. I had forgotten I had any association with the mills at all. The most amazing part of this, for me, was that the next-to-last stage ended within a block of where I'd started (and needed to be), so I was chauffeured to the final in style.

This geocacher did get the point—he or she understands about opening one's heart through geocaching. "It did what this hobby is meant to do—changed my perspective."

May you have many shifts in perception in your hobbies and in your life, and may you always be ready to open your heart.

Wonderful things will happen. I promise.

INTERLUDE

A Conversation with Jeremy Irish

Jeremy Irish is the president and co-founder of Groundspeak, Inc., in Seattle, Washington. Groundspeak owns and operates geocaching.com, the global headquarters for the sport of geocaching.

Why do you geocache?

Nowadays I do it mostly for the exercise or to enjoy hanging out and socializing with other geocachers. Once my son gets old enough I'll start to use it more as a way to enjoy the outdoors with him.

What is your style of caching?

I'm out for a walk in the woods. The usual goal is to go on a high terrain cache hunt. In the Pacific Northwest I have the advantage of having beautiful mountain ranges in almost every direction. Although there is a large selection of caches, I tend to make one or two caches a goal on a longer hike. As a result, my find count remains relatively low.

However, with the recent addition of the geocaching cell phone application, I can do more spontaneous geocaching. I'm pretty bad at preparing for a cache hunt, so this allows me to do it on the spur of the moment. If I am walking my dogs, I can just do a search on my phone and seek one out if it's nearby.

What is the most moving or magical thing that has happened to you when geocaching? Can you share that experience?

I think what amazes me is finding people on the trail who are geocaching at the same time I am. The idea that a largely sedentary activity like the Internet can drive people outside is amazing..This is definitely the motivating factor for running the website.

So seeing a family on the trail who are obviously geocaching, or passing someone on the trail and saying "geocaching?" to them as I pass and seeing the nod, is pretty cool. The same goes for seeing a cache note printed from the website in a cache or reading the entries in a cache logbook. The fact that there are hundreds of thousands of caches being found by people around the world is just mind-boggling.

Do you experience geocaching as being part of a community? If so, in what way(s)? Have people from the community become your friends?

I am mostly a quiet, reserved guy so I like to remain anonymous at events. I do, however, enjoy meeting and talking with geocachers at the events I attend, and enjoy hearing about their experiences. The feedback helps me to "steer" the activity through the geocaching website and create tools to accommodate the needs of the community. It is also a way to get a refreshing insight about the activity from a new or veteran geocacher. After six years of running the website it helps to have a fresh perspective.

What sorts of things do you pick up? What do you leave behind?

With the exception of travel bugs, I hardly ever trade items in caches. I prefer leaving behind detailed logs to talk about my experience visiting the cache location—as well as a log entry on the website. When I do trade items, I usually leave behind something from my favorite place to find cache goodies, Archie McPhee, in Ballard, Washington.

How do you feel when you geocache?

Largely when I go on a hike to find a cache I don't really think much about the cache itself but just appreciate the hike. It is a strong motivator to get me outdoors, but it is really the outdoors I crave—geocaching is often just a means to an end.

Why did you start geocaching.com?

As an IT professional, I realized that technology was chaining me to my home and office. The idea of an activity that takes people outdoors using technology really inspired me to create the website. The unique combination of technology and the outdoors was something that mirrored both of my interests and I thought that it would be popular for others like me.

I hope that activities like geocaching will ultimately bring people back outdoors and away from their home entertainment systems. I don't know if it will happen in my lifetime, but I do hope that as technology gets smaller and more powerful, the culture will change to promote more active lifestyles. As part of other projects at Groundspeak, we hope to support that change through geocaching and other ideas around GPS entertainment.

APPENDIX A

Who Else Caches?

Geocaching.com (along with Groundspeak, its parent company) has, because of being the first to develop the hobby, decidedly exerted a monopoly over it. In some ways this is not good—we've all seen that monopolies do not have to perform well, and so usually do not (a software giant comes immediately to mind even as I use its word processor to write this book). However, it has to be said that, by and large, geocaching.com is run by caring and bright people who emphasize the community aspect of what they do. While any site could have perhaps initially done as well, Groundspeak is the one that succeeded, and with success comes a certain power—or so I believe. It is "the" site one uses if one wants to find organized caches that are well-maintained and in venues that will not hurt the environment while conforming to other guidelines.

While there is no real competition, I would be remiss—particularly as a left-wing, anti-corporate, sometimes-agitator—if I did not indicate the presence of others in the field.

Early in 2006, many websites emerged that listed geocache locations. Some of these had short lives; some had more staying power. The sites that are known as of this writing (with the date they began accepting geocache listings) are as follows:

triax.com/yngwie/gps.html (started May, 2000; now dead)

geocaching.com (Sep, 2000)

geopeitus.ee (Feb, 2001)

navicache.com (Mar, 2001)

geocachingworldwide.com (Jun, 2001; now dead)

geotreasures.com (mid-2001; now dead)

geocaching.hu (?)

geocaching.ru (?)

geogamer.com (Jun, 2002; now dead)

geocaching.gpsgames.org (May, 2004)

terracaching.com (Oct, 2004)

movingcache.com (Dec, 2004; now retired)

geocaching.com.au (Jan, 2005)

opencaching.de (Aug, 2005)

opencaching.pl (Jun, 2006)

APPENDIX B

Like It or Not Puzzle Multi-Cache

An opportunity to visit and then ponder a local poet's life and work.

The point of this puzzle cache is to get you to read some poetry—**like it or not!**

I love poetry, and hope perhaps to interest one or two of you in pursuing it some more.

Please note that to complete this mystery/puzzle cache, you will need to have paper and a ballpoint (not felt-tipped) pen or pencil with you.

You are starting out at Mount Auburn Cemetery, one of my favorite places in the world. Please note that it is closed (and locked) from dusk to dawn. At the listed coordinates is a grouping of graves that includes one family box tomb surrounded by four gravestones that are at ground level. *You do not have to go off the path to find this site. Please do not trample on any plants; this is a botanist's paradise!* You may if you choose purchase a map at the visitor's center.

Should you be interested in this description, please note that a tomb can be a monument commemorating the dead, whether or not the remains are actually inside (as in a vault) or below the ground (as in a grave). A cenotaph is a tomb (again, vault or grave) that contains no remains at all; the remains are elsewhere (lost at sea, buried in a different cemetery, etc.), but a memorial stone is erected in remembrance, usually over a space that would be a grave. In this case, the individual's remains were interred at this site at the time of death; the central feature to this grouping is therefore referred to as a box tomb. (Thanks to Margaret DeAngelis, tapophile, for this information.)

Select the gravestone that has only three lines of information on it.

The picture shows one of the graves in this cluster; use it to make sure you have the correct family, but bear in mind that it is not the grave to be used to decrypt directions to the next cache site—the one you use for decryption has only three lines on it. The following information is to be taken from this gravestone:

First number of the year in the second line

Last number of the year in the second line

Third number of the year in the second line

You should now have three numbers; this is the number of a street address. To obtain the name of the street, continue decoding the directions below, using this same grave:

First letter of the first word in the second line

Third letter of the second word in the first line

First letter of the first word in the first line

Fourth letter of the second word in the second line—twice

Second letter of the first word in the first line

Fifth letter of the first word in the first line

You're almost there! Just to be sure, decrypt the rest of it:

First letter of the second word in the second line

Fourth letter of the second word in the second line

Third letter of the second word in the first line

Fifth letter of the first word in the first line—twice

Fourth letter of the second word in the second line

You should now have a street address in hand! Proceed to that address (note: parking is exceptionally difficult around here, though it is sometimes possible to find a non-resident spot in the oval across the street from the building at the decoded address). This building is in the same city as the original coordinates that you visited above.

If you have the time, the site where you now find yourself is an interesting house to visit with "many layers of history, distinguished architecture, and extensive museum collections (that) reflect the birth and flowering of the nation," though it is only open Wednesdays through Sundays, June through September; there is an admission charge of $3.00 if you are 16 or over. The house is famous for several reasons, one of which is that it served as headquarters for George Washington during the siege of Boston. There is a small garden you can walk through at no charge. *It is not necessary to visit either the house or the grounds to solve this cache.*

You should by now be well acquainted with **Like it or Not**'s theme! But, wait, there's more! Turn your back to the house and look straight ahead of you—and start walking (watching for traffic, of course). You'll first pass through a grass oval surrounded by houses (also a church and the Friends' Society).

Keep walking and you will descend some steps into a park. Take note of the now-familiar bust in this park. You should now still be in a straight line from the house you left.

Now stand in front of the bust and face the river. If you go on a straight line from the bust, through the park gate, and down to the Charles River, you will encounter the cache. It is between the bust and the river going on that straight path through the gate. Be careful crossing the two roads you will encounter!

You do not need to dig to find the cache, and it is in plain sight, though difficult to see. There is no trinket exchange at this cache, and very little space in which to log your entry. The paper is waterproof and *you must bring a ballpoint pen or pencil with you* to write in the log.

You will not be given credit for the cache until you answer the three questions that are in the cache log, email me the answers, and have them approved. If you go ahead and log it without my approval, I will remove your log. This is where I get to make you read poetry—like it or not!

(As a favor to me, please send an email and let me know if the log is getting filled up, so that I can replace it. As you will see, there is very little space available.)

You're probably tired and hungry by now. As you may notice, you're quite close to a famous Square; but, frankly, it has become about as counter-cultural as any mall in the United States (with the added disadvantage that you can't find parking and can get rained on!). Fortunately, there is an independently owned and *very* cool place for beverages and sandwiches or pastries called Darwin, Ltd., nearby at these coordinates: 42 22.452N, 071 07.501W. Maybe you can sit there while you peruse a poetry book for the answers to the log questions!

Special thanks to Paul "NotThePainter" Cézanne for his help, and happy reading!

APPENDIX C

Dark Satanic Mills Multi-Cache with Waypoints

Welcome to the "dark satanic mills" of Manchester, New Hampshire! Take a tour of mill life as you solve this multi-cache and learn about Manchester's past.

> And did those feet in ancient times
> walk upon England's mountains green?
> And was the holy Lamb of God
> on England's pleasant pastures seen?
> And did the countenance divine
> Shine forth upon our clouded hills?
> And was Jerusalem builded here
> Among these dark satanic mills?
>
> (from *Jerusalem* by William Blake)

I've been wanting to do a "mills" cache ever since I moved to Manchester. At one time, the Amoskeag Manufacturing Company was the largest textile manufacturer in the world, and there were thirty thriving mill buildings in Manchester.

This cache will take you on a tour of the mills. You can do it in a car if you're in a hurry, but if you *can* take the time, walking the route will give you a tremendous appreciation for the hopes and dreams, the sweat and the incredible hard work that went into the textile mills of Manchester.

1. **The Overlook:** We'll start at the beginning: the water and the First Nations who lived here. The first Europeans came to settle the Amoskeag in the 1720s, but almost exactly a century before, European explorers had brought with them an epidemic that killed over 90% of the natives in the area. A few Abenaki (a First Nations tribe of the Algonquin language group) remained. We're starting the cache at the Amoskeag Falls, a rich fishing-grounds for the Abenaki and the major reason Manchester was to become an industrial giant—the power of the water.

Note: The starting waypoint is closed from dusk until 7:30AM. It is also closed when PSNH feels like closing it. The view is tremendous and certainly worth waiting for.

This waypoint is at 43 00.072N, 71 28.151W. Enjoy the view, and answer the following question:

On the plaque, the words that follow the title (Overlook) are:

a. the gathering place (E = 449)

b. the place of many fish (E = 362)

c. the place of two canals (E = 507)

d. Neville Point (E = 410)

2. **The Jefferson Mill:** This is the first of several mills you'll see on this tour, and the most elegantly renovated. If you are doing this tour during the day, take a few minutes to step inside: there is a wealth of pictures and artifacts on display in the lobby and corridors that rival the nearby Millyard Museum. If you enter through the clocktower entrance, go past the elevator and continue exploring to your right: you'll have the opportunity to get a sense of just how large this building really is.

The waypoint is at 42 59.838N, 71 28.093W. Imagine the hundreds of people working this mill (in summer, windows had to be closed to prevent contamination of the cloth—just imagine how hot it was!) and answer the following question:

How many white circular caution signs are on the building facing Commercial Street?

a. 6 (F = 15)

b. 5 (F = 222)

c. 8 (F = 110)

d. 16 (F = 28)

3. **The Mill Girl:** This famous statue commemorates the women who worked the mills. This was the first opportunity for many women to get out of the house and earn money on their own, and the opportunity proved irresistible to many. Women became supervisors and one of them, Margaret Knight, became an inventor after witnessing a fatal accident involving a spindle; she went on to create and patent a number of inventions in the textile industry.

The waypoint is at 42 59.499N, 71 28.041W. Imagine all the girls from Québec and Ireland flocking to Manchester in order to earn a living working the mills, and answer the following question:

What entrance is to the right of the plaque?

a. North (G = 50)

b. South (G = 56)

c. Service (G = 64)

d. Main (G = 139)

4. **The Last Undeveloped Mill:** In contrast to the beauty of the present-day Jefferson Mill, this mill building—the last to be in use manufacturing textiles—has suffered a number of setbacks, not least of which a fire in 2005 that gutted the unoccupied building.

The waypoint is at 42 59.230N, 71 28.149W. There is a sign here that used to be on top of the building. It reads:

a. Wambec (H = 14)

b. Pandora (H = 17)

c. Stark (H = 20)

d. Amoskeag (H = 23)

5. **Worker Housing:** Until 1920, Manchester was a "strikeless city;" the workers identified with the corporation, and the latter provided them with amenities that kept unions away. These amenities included healthcare, children's recreation, home ownership opportunities, a textile club, a library, and classes. Much of the housing offered by the AMC, conveniently located near the mills, is still in use, some renovated better than others.

The waypoint is at 42 59.365N, 71 27.920W. You're now on West Merrimack Street. When heading down West Merrimack from Elm Street toward Canal Street, note the first building on your right after the *second* parking lot on your right. It is number:

a. 97 (J = 91)

b. 62 (J = 310)

c. 88 (J = 124)

d. 153 (J = 33)

6. **Millyard Museum:** If you are doing this cache during the day, by all means visit the Millyard Museum and learn more about the city's history. (Free passes to the museum are available to Manchester residents at the Manchester City Library). Here you'll learn about the canals and the hydro-power that made the mills possible; the great flywheel disaster; the ambience of a "company city" (all shops were open late on Thursday nights, for example—since Thursday was payday at the AMC). You'll also see how the com-

pany's amenities finally ceased to be enough when between 1841 and 1845 mill workers' workloads were increased, but pay was cut twice, actions seen by the workers as a betrayal of trust. The strikes began and the mills never recovered; the AMC mills shut down for good on Christmas Eve, 1935.

The waypoint is at 42 59.382N, 71 28.058W. There is a large number on the clock tower here. That number is:

  a. 26 (K = 0)

  b. 6 (K = 45)

  c. 13 (K = 92)

  d. 3 (K = 18)

7. **The Final: le petit Canada:** Congratulations! Now you can relax and enjoy the view of the river that made the local industrial revolution possible. Here too you're facing the area where a whole community of workers from Québec established "le petit Canada" and where to this day you can still go and eat *poutine*! (Note: you cannot actually see the restaurant where you can eat poutine, or indeed le petit Canada from this site; you're not *in* that part of town: you're merely looking in that direction and using your imagination!)

The cache is located at:

42 59.L (where L = E + F + G)

71 28.M (where M = H + J + K)

The cache is a logbook-only cache, so bring your own pencil, ballpoint pen or sharpie. It may be wet but the logbook is made of waterproof paper.

Additional Reading

There is much more to learn about the mills and both the amazing technical advances made as well as some of the poignant stories of child labor, long labor, and xenophobia. If you'd like to learn more, the Images of America series has a great book called *Manchester: The Mills and the Immigrant Experience,* by Gary Samson; the Postcard History Series gives great images of the city (and its many floods!) in *Manchester* by Robert Perrault; and hit either the library, amazon.com, or the gift shop at the Millyard Museum for the most in-depth look at the mills: *Amoskeag: Life and Work in an American Factory-City,* by Tamara Hareven and Randolph Langenbach.

Additional Waypoints

AA   JEFFER   Jefferson Mill (Question to Answer)
N 42° 59.838 W 071° 28.093

BB   MILGRL   Mill Girl (Question to Answer)
N 42° 59.499 W 071° 28.041

CC   LASTUN   Last Undeveloped Mill (Question to Answer)
N 42° 59.230 W 071° 28.149

DD   HOUSNG   Worker Housing (Question to Answer)
N 42° 59.365 W 071° 27.920

EE   MILLYD   Millyard Museum (Question to Answer)
N 42° 59.382 W 071° 28.058

Bread and Roses Geo-Events

Good friends, good (and cheap) food in a smoke-free environment in Manchester, New Hampshire

We so enjoyed The Constabulary Capers Revisited that we wanted to bring the merriment north to Manchester. Please join us for a sharing of "life's glories" at the *Bread and Roses Manchester Geo-Event!* (*Bread and Roses* is now a periodic event; it will occur every four months in February, June, and October on the first Wednesday of the month.)

The event is held at The Shaskeen (theshaskeen.com; please visit the website for the next date). The venue has a back room; that's where we'll be. This is a smoke-free environment. We've told the pub that we'll be arriving around 6pm but feel free to trickle in; it would help the wait-staff. The pub closes at 9:45 P.M. Prices are very reasonable.

Street parking is pretty easy in Manchester, but you'll need a quarter for a half hour on the meter before 8 P.M. There is a large lot at 42 59.596N 071 27.635W. The entrance to the lot says "Permit Only" but the spaces say, "Permit before 5:30 P.M." I'm also sure you'll find a metered space closer than that!

There is no need to say whether you are eating or drinking ahead of time. The Shaskeen wait-staff certainly has proved their ability to handle anything we can throw at them.

There will be a TB swap table (but no log) and we're hoping to get some swag raffled off, but we'll see how generous the manufacturers are.

And Now a Word from Our Sponsors:

We have three sponsors this year: backcountry.com, garmin.com, and our returning sponsor, shop.groundspeak.com. The cardboard boxes full of goodies have already started arriving! We would like to thank these generous companies for donating merchandise to give away!

Bread and Roses

As we come marching, marching in the beauty of the day,
A million darkened kitchens, a thousand mill lofts gray,
Are touched with all the radiance that a sudden sun discloses,
For the people hear us singing: "Bread and roses! Bread
     and roses!"
As we come marching, marching, we battle too for men,
For they are women's children, and we mother them again.
Our lives shall not be sweated from birth until life closes;
Hearts starve as well as bodies; give us bread, but give us roses!
As we come marching, marching, unnumbered women dead
Go crying through our singing their ancient cry for bread.
Small art and love and beauty their drudging spirits knew.
Yes, it is bread we fight for - but we fight for roses, too!
As we come marching, marching, we bring the greater days.
The rising of the women means the rising of the race.
No more the drudge and idler - ten that toil where one reposes,
But a sharing of life's glories: Bread and roses! Bread and roses!

—James Oppenheim

In 2005 we moved to Manchester and were immediately fascinated with its history. First Nations tribes had already made the rich fishing site a village; but as the Industrial Age progressed, men with money also saw the potential of the Merrimack River and designed a city that would become, and remain for many years, a corporation town.

That corporation was the Amoskeag Manufacturing Company, and at one time there was not a resident of Manchester who did not owe his or her living in some way to the corporation. The Amoskeag mill complex was the largest in the world, the ever-expanding job opportunities bringing women into the workforce and attracting immigrants from Canada, Ireland, and Greece. There was also the dark side to the mills' long hours, child labor, and poor working conditions. The next time you pass by a mill building - any mill building - look hard at the rows of long windows. They were closed, all the time, so that nothing could contaminate the textiles being manufactured. Imagine working in such a room in the summer: the heat magnified by the glass, the deafening roar of the machines, asking permission to leave the room to use the bathroom - and not getting that permission. Blake described well the "dark, satanic mills" of the nineteenth and early twentieth century.

But the twentieth century did bring some hope. A number of movements aimed at bettering the lives of various groups of people were making themselves heard. One such movement, demanding the rights of women to vote, inspired a song titled *Bread and Roses*.

The song was soon taken up by textile workers in Lawrence, Massachusetts, who had recently voted to go on strike. After World War One, the realization had been made that it was cheaper and more efficient to locate textile mills in the south, near where the cotton is harvested. New England mills responded to the competition by lowering wages, increasing hours, and making the mills more dangerous places to work. In response to these impossible working conditions, workers went on strikes all over New England, unintentionally yet effectively closing down the mills forever. The Amoskeag survived the strikes of 1922, but closed its doors forever in the 1930s. Manchester has only in the past twenty years begun to rebound from the economic depression caused by the closing of the mills.

We chose *Bread and Roses* as our theme for this event because of its connection with the history of our city, with the terrible times that preceded the strikes; but also because we connected with what it expressed. We all need bread. . . but we desire roses. That little extra something in life can be called a hobby, something that is unnecessary for survival but which brings joy. Some of us call that geocaching.

MuchAdo (Mike Berger) says—*If you look at the bottom picture on the event page, in the center you'll see two round spools at the base of the two looms—those are called beams. They feed the yarn to the looms. My high school job (back in the 70's) was to remove the empty ones (like those in the picture) and replace them with full ones. When they were full with cotton yarn, they were relatively light—500–800 lbs. But with synthetics, they could get up to 2,500 lbs. We used manual "trucks" with a hand pumped hydraulic lift to move them and load them into the looms. I was quite muscular by the time I left that job to go off to college!*

The picture of the women is the area where they put the yarn on the beams—I forget the name for that area. They are surrounded by the individual strands of yarn—an "end." Each strand is fed through those racks and wound up onto a beam. A beam would typically have between 60 and 360 ends.

APPENDIX E

Additional Resources

Possibly the best resource you can use is the geocaching.com site. The second best is Cacheopedia, a wiki site that is a combination encyclopedia, resource tool, and survival guide about geocaching. Use it as you would Wikipedia, with the same disclaimers: no one is policing the site, so errors can creep in. That said, however, it's a great place to learn more. Cacheopedia can be found online at cacheopedia.com/wiki/Main_Page.

Books

All of the books noted have something to offer, and if you like to read, by all means, go out and try one or two of them. The real *problem* is that there aren't many offering information that you cannot already find on the geocaching.com website. There are more illustrations, yes; there are some cool anecdotes and so on; but I wouldn't trust any of the books to recommend technology, for example, since it's moving too fast for print publications to keep up.

Frankly, though, if you want to find the most recent information about a hobby that is still in its infancy and therefore growing rapidly, my recommendation (sorry, fellow authors) is to stick with the websites.

On the other hand, I'm including a number of books about finding your joy in the outdoors, about looking up, about breathing; those are timeless.

Brady, Bernard and Mark Neuzil: *A Spiritual Field Guide: Meditations for the Outdoors,* Grand Rapids, Michigan: Brazos Books (a division of Baker Books), 2005. I'll confess: this book surprised me. While it is drawing from a historic Christian tradition, it pulls the reader into reflections by Augustine, Thérèse of Lisieux, and Annie Dillard, while at the same time opening a door into the beauty and richness of nature, something in which mainstream Christianity has historically shown little interest. Well-written . . . and my copy, at least, is now well-annotated and well-underlined, too!

Cameron, Laine: *The Geocaching Handbook,* Old Saybrook, Connecticut: Falcon Books (a division of Pequot Press), 2004. I have to say that this book has the coolest cover of any of the geocaching books, but it really is only for absolute beginners. My sense is that if you've finished my book, even with its lapses in the practical details department, you'll be ready for something with more content than offered here, even if it *is* offered by Dave Ulmer himself.

Depriest, Dale: *A GPS User Manual: Working with Garmin Receivers,* Bloomington, Indiana: Authorhouse, 2003. Both specialized and dated.

Dyer, Mike: *The Essential Guide to Geocaching: Tracking Treasure With Your GPS,* Golden, Colorado: Fulcrum Publishing, 2004. Another "essential" guide. Dyer does, however, bring a certain expertise to the table, as he is himself a geographer and cartographer; the book is concise yet really does have something for everyone. Well worth checking out.

Hall, Randy: *The Letterboxer's Companion,* Old Saybrook, Connecticut: Falcon Books (a division of Pequot Press), 2003. A quick read that covers the essentials (including how to carve your own letterboxing stamp!). The book is also gorgeous and makes a terrific gift.

Hinch, Stephen: *Outdoor Navigation with GPS,* Mendocino, California: Annadel Press, 2004. What's really nice about this book is that it provides backup navigation techniques so that if your GPS unit fails you'll still be able to find your way home. This publisher (annadelpress.com) is well worth checking out: all the company produces are books about GPS. If that's your area of interest, this is the publisher for you.

McNamara, Joel: *Geocaching for Dummies*, Hoboken, NJ: Wiley Publishing, Inc, 2004. Quick and to the point, the Dummies entry for geocaching. Has a lot of information about group geocaching activities.

McNamara, Joel: *GPS For Dummies*, Hoboken, NJ: Alpha Books, 2004. Offers great information (certainly more than I ever wanted to know about my GPS unit!), but that same pesky problem is still present, in that it's already dated. Still, if you want to have something to carry around (as opposed to a laptop) that will teach you how to use the device, it's a reasonable purchase. Otherwise, again, the information on the web is more up-to-date.

Nhat Hanh, Thich: *Walking Meditation*, Louisville, Colorado: Sounds True Publishing, 2006. This is available in hardcover and as a DVD to listen to when you're walking. While not strictly about forests or geocaching, it will help you find a rhythm of meditating as you walk—slowly, this isn't orienteering!—through a beautiful place.

Owings, Rich: *GPS Mapping*, Fort Bragg, California: Ten Mile Press, 2005. Several of the amazon reviews are extremely positive about this book.

Peters, Jack: *The Complete Idiot's Guide to Geocaching*, New York, NY: Alpha Books, 2004. This book was partly written by the Groundspeak staff and is excellent: use it as your starter kit.

Sherman, Eric: Geocaching: *Hike and Seek with Your GPS*, New York, NY: Apress Books, 2006. I like this one even better than either the Dummies or the Idiot's Guide books. It's clear, straightforward, and gives you a lot of information about being out in the woods. Excellent book.

Thorp, Gary: *Caught in Fading Light: Mountain Lions, Zen Masters, and Wild Nature*, New York, New York: Walker Books (a division of Bloomsbury Publishing), 2002. When you're looking for something, that journey can change the way you see everything. It's an apt metaphor for geocaching and a simply wonderful book.

Websites

Remember that websites come and go. It's the nature of the Net. Some are temporarily disabled because of a bug or because of a site update that didn't update all the pages; some just disappear permanently for a myriad number of reasons. All of these links were alive and well when this book went to press, but you're on your own after that. If a URL doesn't work, or if you don't remember it, try typing the site or page name into a search engine and see if it can't help you find the site, or at least a similar one. It's why I've included the titles here—it gives you a better chance of connecting.

Armchair Treasure Hunt Club (treasureclub.net): A UK-based club that circulates clues to finding hidden or buried "treasure."

Bookcrossing (bookcrossing.com): Books just want to be free! Find out how to catch and release them at Bookcrossing, a site that tracks books as they pass from reader to reader.

Buxley's Geocaching Waypoint (brillig.com/geocaching): Sometimes in synch with Groundspeak, sometimes desperately out of synch, Buxley maintains a site that is interesting and an alternative to geocaching.com. He keeps a list of Scavenger Hunt Caches that is fun to check out.

Degree Confluence Project (confluence.org): Is in the process of amassing pictures from all the confluence points on the planet. Try your hand at it or just see what others are doing.

First 100 Geocaches (members.cox.net/pkpublic/index.html): the world's oldest hundred geocaches, where they are/were, status (active or archived), and more.

Fizzymagic's Geocaching Site (fizzymagic.net/Geocaching/index.html): This is a geek site offering geocaching applications, tools, and "other geocaching stuff."

Fuzzy's Geocaching Page O'Wonders (parkrrrr.com): The dean, as it were, of Geocaching University put up this page to point visitors to a number of Fuzzy's own utilities, organized around the programs with which the utilities work.

Geocacher University (geocacher-u.com): This is a terrific site with the same basic information that can be found elsewhere, but with really useful articles as well. As I'm writing, the current headline article is about writing: Writing Great Online Logs ("For many people, posting their geocaching finds online constitutes their first endeavor in creative writing and online publishing." Okay, so it's a little wordy—but the article content is good). Also includes micro-cache labels. A terrific place to explore.

Geocaching Swiss Army Knife—GSAK (gsak.net): an all-in-one geocaching and waypoint management tool, used by most of the people I know who geocache. GSAK (pronounced gee-sack) offers "multiple databases, sending/receiving waypoints to GPSr, conversion to many mapping formats, HTML output, extensive searching, macro support, backup and restore, distance/direction from other waypoints (including caches, locations, post codes) and much more." It's free to check out but you need to pay for it after 21 days.

GeoChecker (geochecker.com) application that allows you to verify you have the correct solution to a geocache puzzle before actually going to the location and searching for the cache.

GeoLex (geolex.locusprime.net): The best geocaching glossary out there. It contains terms and acronyms I would never have been able to figure out, as well as lots of entries that had my mouth slightly open (people do that?).

GPS Information (gpsinformation.net): If you're trying to determine which GPS to buy, what features you needs, and where to buy at a discount, hardware and software reviews, and more, this site is for you! Check it out for everything GPS.

GPS Visualizer (gpsvisualizer.com): A free, easy-to-use online utility that creates maps and profiles from GPS data (tracks and waypoints), street addresses, or simple coordinates.

Keenpeople.com (keenpeople.com): An open community of GPS users, hikers, geocachers, outdoor enthusiasts, and friends.

Monkey Cache (monkeycache.com): Um, I think that's all I have to say about this one.

National Geodetic Survey (ngs.noaa.gov): "NOAA's National Geodetic Survey (NGS) defines and manages a national coordinate system. This network, the National Spatial Reference System (NSRS), provides the foundation for transportation and communication; mapping and charting; and a multitude of scientific and engineering applications. Committed to making transportation and navigation safer, NGS conducts aerial photography surveys near airports in the United States and its possessions to position obstructions and aids to air travel. NGS also maps the coastal regions of the United States and provides data for navigational charts. NGS develops Federal standards for geodetic surveys and helps to coordinate surveying methods. NGS State Geodetic Advisors are stationed in several states to work with local communities to expand surveying capabilities." (taken from website)

Photo Tag (phototag.org): People brought together through "the chance wandering of transient disposable cameras." People are instructed to take one picture and pass the camera on. What fun!

Texas Geocaching (texasgeocaching.com/index.asp): The name says it all.

Today's Cacher (todayscacher.com): this is Jerry Carter's online geocaching magazine, with fresh articles, event notifications, a section on cool caches, humor, and other features. Check it out! Jerry is also the creator of the wonderful geocaching hiking staffs mentioned earlier in this book and which can be seen at geo-hikingstick.com.

Update to the Geocaching FAQ (markwell.us/geofaq.htm): Team Markwell, bless them, have decided to update the geocaching website's frequently asked questions section by prowling around on the forums, seeing what questions people really are asking frequently, and putting them together on this website.

Utah Cache Games (cachunuts.com): The site's tagline is "Discover Utah—One Cache at a Time!" One state's effort to get people involved in what I earlier called geo-tourism.

Where's George? (wheresgeorge.com): Tracks U.S. currency by serial number. The cool thing is that the CDC actually used the database to see how money flows in order to work out disease vectors!

APPENDIX F

Glossary

There are a whole lot of acronyms and language specific to geo-caching, so this, too, may be a tear-out page for you. Or at least a well-read one until you're up to speed with this particular jargon!

Archive: A cache can be removed from being listed on the geo-caching site for a number of different reasons. It can be temporarily disabled (not archived), if it needs maintenance or if there's a prob-lem (I had to temporarily archive *Dark Satanic Mills* when the cache container disappeared and I couldn't replace it for a week or so). It can be permanently archived when it is over (as in an event) or when the owner decides that he/she no longer wants to take responsibility for it. When Paul and I move to Canada, we will either archive all our local caches or offer them for adoption by other geocachers.

Bookmarks: A way for a geocacher to keep track of things that are not part of geocaching.com's tracking system. You can use book-marks to record anything you want—FTFs, favorite caches, etc. Paul's "best caches" bookmark list can be seen at tinyurl.com/ yjvhok, and his FTFP bookmark list is at tinyurl.com/yfjfhd (I'm using Paul's pages as an example since I don't bookmark anything myself . . . if I write about what happens in the woods or on caching trips, it's generally much longer, much more personal, and goes into my journal or winds up as an essay somewhere!). You'll need to be registered with geocaching.com to access these pages.

CCCooperAgency: Famous in geocaching circles and referred to in Sue's interview, CCCooperAgency is a geocacher who has amassed extraordinary geocaching numbers: as of this writing, 474 caches hidden, 17,438 caches found, 1378 hitchhikers passed along, 150 hitchhikers "owned."

CITO: Cache-In-Trash-Out. Every geocacher tries to practice CITO whenever he or she goes out into the wild. There are also organized CITO events in areas that appear to require a concerted effort.

DNF: Did not find.

FTF: First-to-Find, the first geocacher to locate and log a cache. There are FTF "hounds" who have notifications sent to them as soon as a new cache goes "live" in their area and race each other to the find—be it at eleven at night or four in the morning. There is often a special prize waiting in the geocache for the FTF it, and it's one of the statistics that you can maintain on the geocaching website through bookmarks. From Cacheopedia: "Many cachers keep a separate count of their FTFs, and regional caching groups often have competition for who has the most FTFs within a geographic area. Although the person(s) who physically first find the cache may not be the first to get online and report the find, by definition, the FTF goes to the person(s) whose name is at the top of the logsheet. Terracaches take it a step further and offer a separate code to confirm who was the First To Find. Some caches include a special swag item for the FTF person. With a little creativity, this can be done in all sizes of containers. We set a micro near a new movie theater and put a five-dollar gift certificate to the theater as the FTF prize."

FTFP: First-to-Find-Published: yes, Virginia, there's a way to circumvent the assumptions made by geocaching's originators. Paul was frustrated by someone in our area accessing and logging caches before their actual publication, so (in typical Paul fashion) instead of fretting about it, he had a Zen moment and realized that he and the other geocacher were simply playing different games. He coined the FTFP to define the way that he plays.

Here is how people have been able to find a cache *before* it is published:

1. When a travel bug is dropped into an unpublished cache. People do it all the time because they don't know they shouldn't. If you are watching the bug, you can see the distance and approximate direction it moved from its last spot. This lets you know approximately where it is—which is often good enough for the persistent and it is especially good enough during the winter when you can follow footprints in the snow.

2. There is a bug in the old geocaching WAP site; the bug was fixed in the new site but the old site was never taken down. WAP is the protocol that small devices (like cell phones and PDAs) use for web access. This bug lets you find caches with extreme accuracy as long as the cache has been approved for a delayed publication, like the *Bread and Roses* caches, for example.

Global Positioning System (GPS): The only fully functional satellite navigation system. More than two dozen GPS satellites broadcast precise timing signals to GPS receivers; these signals allow the receiver to pinpoint its exact location on the planet.

GPSr: Abbreviation used to indicate the GPS receiver. Also sometimes called GPS devices or GPS units.

GZ: Ground zero—where the coordinates displayed on your GPSr match closely those of the listed coordinates for the cache. As noted earlier, this is where the hunt *really* begins! (Hint: Put your backpack down on what the GPS receiver says is ground zero, so that as you wander around looking for the cache, you don't go too far away.)

Hitchhiker: An object or item that is meant to travel from cache to cache. Hitchhikers include travel bugs, geocoins, etc. Most of them are Groundspeak-branded, though they do not have to be. Travelertags.com is another site that addresses hitchhikers.

Latitude: The distance north to south from the earth's equator. Along with longitude, it's used by a GPS receiver to compute the location of a cache or of a waypoint.

Letterboxing: An activity similar to geocaching but not using technology; letterboxers locate their caches through written directions in their language of choice. In many ways the parent activity to geocaching, letterboxing began

Longitude: The east/west distance in degrees as measured from Greenwich, England.

Podcacher (podcacher.com): A weekly family-friendly geocaching podcast. I haven't tried it out, but it looks like a lot of fun!

PQ: Pocket Query, a downloadable file in .gpx format listing waypoints, descriptions, and encryped hints, is used commonly for paperless caching with a PDA. (A .gpx file is used for many things. You can load it into you PDA. However, the most common use is to load it into GSAK and use GSAK's features to select which caches you will load into your GPSr.)

SBA: Should Be Archived; cache is placed in a dangerous or prohibited location, is missing, etc.

SIG: Abbreviation for signatures, or signature items, that may be left in a cache to personalize a geocacher's visit.

Signal the Frog: The official geocaching mascot. Signal is available via Groundspeak's store in any number of incarnations and is a sure way for geocachers to recognize each other.

Signature Items: Items that are particular to one geocacher and that are consistently left in caches visited by that cacher. They can be keychains, toys, sports cards, etc.

SWAG: Stuff We All Get, or treasure/trinkets left in or taken from a cache.

TFTC!: Thanks For The Cache!

TNLN: Took Nothing, Left Nothing. What many geocachers do when they want to simply find the cache, write in the log, and enjoy the area. This should be noted in the logbook; some geocachers like to keep up with what is flowing in and out of their cache.

TNLNSL: Took Nothing, Left Nothing, Signed Log. I always found this a little redundant (after all, if I'm writing TNLN in the log it's pretty clear that I signed the log), but I'm more of a purist with the language than are most people.

Travel Bug (TB): A hitchhiker with Groundspeak tags attached for tracking, and a goal sheet attached for details about its travels.

Watch list: You can sign up to "watch" any cache. Logs that are recorded online are then sent to you. I like watching my own (which you do automatically—you don't sign up for watching your own); others keep a list of caches they watch. Paul maintains a far more extensive watch list than I do, and when I asked him what he watches, he responded, "I watch all caches that are brand new so I can scope out the FTFP competition. I also used to watch every single cache I've ever found so I could vicariously enjoy other's caching experiences and compare them to my own, but I've cut back on that. I also watch the first TB we ever found (Leif Erikson) because it reminds me of you!"

Waypoint (WP or WPT): A named coordinate (latitude/longitude) that locates a point on the earth. You can place several waypoints along the way to your cache as necessary. From the geocachin.com site: "Geocaching uses a suggested waypoint for a cache, created automatically when a cache has been created. Because most GPS units have restricted names to 6 characters or less, we generate a waypoint name based on the ID of the cache. It is optional, but makes it easier to locate a cache on the geocaching website."

Index

About the Author

 **Jeannette Cézanne** is a writer and editor who divides her time between Manchester, New Hampshire, and Provincetown, Massachusetts. She has published fiction under a number of different pen names, and is president of Customline Wordware, Inc., a company providing business, marketing, and literary writing and editing services to corporate and individual clients.

Jeannette is married to Paul (NotThePainter) Cézanne and has two stepchildren, Jacob (NotYourName) and Anastasia (Animal-Cacher) Czarnecki.

She spends most of her time learning how to do some of the things she talks about in this book: breathing, looking up, finding her joy. It's an ongoing journey.

Contests, new titles, events, news, discussion
and feedback. Sign up for your latest chance
to win, and find out about upcoming books at
www.dreamtimepublishing.com

OUR COMMUNITY

DreamTime Publishing supports the community by
participating regularly in worthwhile fundraising and
charitable efforts. Let us know what's important to you,
and sign up at **www.dreamtimepublishing.com**
to find out what's happening near you.

ONLINE BOOK CLUB AND MORE!

Come by and share in a discussion of the latest books
from top authors and leave your feedback on
DreamTime Publishing's titles and for our authors.
Sign up at **www.dreamtimepublishing.com**
to get the latest information.

WHAT'S GOING ON?

Check out our online calendar for events
and appearances by DreamTime authors.
Sign up at **www.dreamtimepublishing.com**
to make sure you don't miss anything!